Chatgpt

A Quick-start Guide to Effective Ai Use

(Complete Guide to Chatgpt From Beginners to Experts)

Kenneth Escoto

Published By **Darby Connor**

Kenneth Escoto

Chatgpt: A Quick-start Guide to Effective Ai Use (Complete Guide to Chatgpt From Beginners to Experts)

ISBN   978-1-7770663-9-0

No part of this guidebook shall be reproduced in any form without permission in writing from the publisher except in the case of brief quotations embodied in critical articles or reviews.

Legal & Disclaimer

The information contained in this book is not designed to replace or take the place of any form of medicine or professional medical advice. The information in this book has been provided for educational & entertainment purposes only.

The information contained in this book has been compiled from sources deemed reliable, and it is accurate to the best of the Author's knowledge; however, the Author cannot guarantee its accuracy and validity and cannot be held liable for any errors or omissions. Changes are periodically made to this book. You must consult your doctor or get professional medical advice before using any of the suggested remedies, techniques, or information in this book.

Table Of Contents

Chapter 1: Benefits Of Chatgpt Inside The Workplace

1. Increased productivity

ChatGPT can appreciably beautify productiveness within the place of business by way of manner of using automating obligations that would normally require a massive amount of effort and time. For instance, ChatGPT can robotically reply to emails, schedule appointments, or maybe generate files. By delegating those responsibilities to ChatGPT, employees can attention on their middle abilities and have extra time for greater hard obligations.

2. Improved selection-making

ChatGPT can also help in choice-making in the expert context. By reading and evaluating huge volumes of information, ChatGPT can provide precious insights and facts that can beneficial beneficial resource in selection-making. For instance, ChatGPT can assist understand dangers and possibilities or create forecasts concerning destiny traits.

3. Enhanced verbal exchange

ChatGPT also can make a contribution to improving communique within the place of job. For example, employees can use ChatGPT to talk with each extraordinary brief and effectively, minimizing misunderstandings. ChatGPT also can help overcome language limitations thru mechanically translating texts into different languages.

four. Enhanced time manage

ChatGPT can beautify time management with the resource of supporting inside the making plans and business enterprise of workflows. For example, ChatGPT can assist create schedules and allocate responsibilities to make certain well timed finishing touch. ChatGPT also can useful beneficial resource in tracking and updating project improvement to make certain smooth operations.

five. Increased performance

ChatGPT can beautify performance within the place of job. By automating repetitive obligations, employees can employ their time extra efficaciously and popularity on more hard obligations. ChatGPT also can assist enhance the accuracy of duties thru lowering errors and improving the super of hard work.

6. Enhanced customer support

Overall customer support in agencies may be superior by manner of ChatGPT. For example, ChatGPT can assist in all of sudden and efficaciously responding to consumer inquiries thru mechanically addressing regularly asked questions. ChatGPT also can beneficial resource in personalizing purchaser research through way of accumulating and the use of records approximately clients' selections and needs.

7. Enhanced competitiveness

In contemporary competitive business commercial enterprise organization surroundings, businesses want to distinguish themselves from their competition. ChatGPT can assist organizations decorate their competitiveness with the aid of way of giving them an part in automating business enterprise approaches and studying data. Companies the use of ChatGPT can respond to changes more all at once and make higher alternatives than their competition, essential to a aggressive advantage.

eight. Cost financial savings

The implementation of ChatGPT can also result in huge charge monetary savings by using manner of automating workflows and growing productiveness. For instance, businesses can hire ChatGPT to automate customer service duties, ensuing in monetary economic savings on employees costs, or lessen errors and downtime, most critical to monetary financial savings on upkeep expenses.

nine. Improved worker delight

By automating repetitive and time-consuming obligations, ChatGPT can help lessen the workload of employees. This can bring about higher employee pleasure and a better work-existence stability. ChatGPT also can make contributions to improving the artwork environment with the useful resource of facilitating communique and collaboration amongst personnel.

10. Improved Data Security

By the usage of ChatGPT, agencies can also beautify their statistics protection. ChatGPT can contribute to defensive the records of corporations via implementing safety protocols and preventing unauthorized get entry to to statistics. ChatGPT also can assist in complying with records protection pointers via automatically figuring out and managing touchy information because it need to be.

eleven. Generating passive profits

Last but not least, the use of ChatGPT lets in human beings, specifically those operating from domestic or in self-employment, to generate a strong passive earnings. Some of the incomes possibilities furnished in this manual, which incorporates online surveys, accomplice advertising and marketing, or textual content and content material cloth creation, are fantastic for constructing an prolonged-term passive earnings flow into.

In precis, ChatGPT offers many blessings in the expert sphere, starting from progressed productivity and average overall performance to progressed desire-making and worker pride. Companies that use ChatGPT can beautify their competitiveness, keep costs, enhance facts safety, and reduce the workload on their employees.

II. Revolution ChatGPT –

How works what?

What exactly is ChatGPT?

ChatGPT is a captivating instance of the improvement of synthetic intelligence. As a form of "virtual assistant," ChatGPT may have interaction with humans, solution questions, provide recommendation, or even keep conversations.

ChatGPT is the surrender quit result of years of studies and development at OpenAI, one of the primary agencies in the challenge of synthetic intelligence. The idea within the again of the challenge changed into to create a gadget that is able to communicating with humans in a herbal manner, while having human-like conversations.

The gadget is based totally completely at the GPT-4.Zero shape, a in addition improvement of the GPT-3.Five model from OpenAI. The abbreviation "GPT" stands for "Generative Pretrained Transformer". This is a shape of neural community that is professional with a big quantity of facts. In this manner, the version is capable of react to a huge amount of inputs and generate corresponding outputs.

ChatGPT schooling is completed with the useful resource of analyzing big quantities of texts, which includes books, articles, and on line content material material. The model uses this statistics to recognize and recognize styles and relationships in speech. In this way, ChatGPT learns to have human-like conversations and respond to complicated queries.

The gadget is able to being used in plenty of extremely good areas. For instance, ChatGPT may be used as a virtual assistant in businesses or as a help agent in customer support departments. The device also can be useful in training or healthcare to help pupils, college college students or sufferers.

Another advantage of ChatGPT is that it's far constantly being evolved. By training with new data and adapting the algorithms, the system can turn out to be better and higher and be prolonged to a big sort of applications.

However, there are also important voices that warn of the capacity effect of ChatGPT and similar structures. For instance, jobs in customer service or first-rate regions want to get replaced by manner of manner of automation. There is also a risk that the machine will by twist of fate reproduce prejudices or discrimination, as it is informed on the premise of cutting-edge information.

Overall, however, ChatGPT is a charming example of the improvement of synthetic intelligence and has the functionality to change many areas of our lives.

The version can be used on one in every of a kind systems and thru one-of-a-type media. For example, it's miles feasible to engage with ChatGPT via messaging apps or internet web sites. Voice assistants inclusive of Siri or Alexa additionally use comparable technology to speak with customers.

Working with ChatGPT

There are nearly endless possibilities how ChatGPT may be used inside the career for aid. We would really like to proportion some examples with you right here.

1. Content creation

ChatGPT may be used to create content material for blogs, net sites, social media structures or on line courses. You can sell the created content material fabric or use it for advertising and marketing and advertising income.

2. Marketing and advertising and marketing campaigns

ChatGPT can help increase and optimize advertising and advertising and marketing and advertising and marketing campaigns for businesses. You can paintings as a consultant for corporations or create your very personal campaigns and promote them to companies.

3. Text correction and optimization

ChatGPT may be used for textual content correction and search engine advertising optimization. You can artwork right here as a freelancer for businesses or provide your very own correction and optimization offerings.

four. Chatbot Development

ChatGPT can be used to expand chatbots for businesses. You can work as a developer for businesses or expand your very very own chatbots and promote them to corporations.

5. Translation offerings

ChatGPT can be used to translate texts into one of a kind languages. You can art work as a freelancer for groups or offer your very personal translation offerings.

6. Data acquisition and analysis

ChatGPT can be used to build up and take a look at facts in diverse industries. Here, you may artwork as a facts analyst for groups or offer your very private records analysis services.

7. Chatbot verbal exchange introduction

ChatGPT can assist create and optimize dialogs for chatbots. You can paintings as a freelancer for businesses or offer your very own services for developing chatbot dialogs.

There are many strategies ChatGPT can be used within the profession to earn coins. However, it is predicated upon at the abilties and expertise of the individual what form of services they could offer.

Applications in exercise

Complementing the previously mentioned makes use of of ChatGPT, beneath are 10 particular examples of sensible makes use of of ChatGPT.

1. Customer Service

ChatGPT may be used in customer service to answer client questions speedy and effectively. This lets in companies to provide customer support in the course of the clock and reply to purchaser queries speedy.

2. Education

ChatGPT may be carried out in education to aid scholars and college college students. For instance, questions on sure topics can be replied or ChatGPT can assist with getting to know via way of giving feedback or providing information.

three.   Healthcare

ChatGPT may be utilized in healthcare to reply affected character questions or offer medical statistics. This manner, sufferers may be supported quicker and greater efficaciously.

four.   Travel Management

ChatGPT can be applied in adventure management to answer questions about flight times, resort bookings or itineraries. This manner, travelers can be supported faster and further successfully.

5.   Finance

ChatGPT may be used in the subject of finance to reply questions about debts, transfers or funding techniques. This manner, customers can be supported quick and correctly.

6.   Human resources

ChatGPT may be applied in human assets to reply employees' questions or provide information approximately operating situations and rules.

7. Entertainment

ChatGPT additionally may be used in the entertainment enterprise to engage with lovers of celebrities or athletes or to provide video games and quizzes.

8. Marketing

ChatGPT may be applied in advertising to reply customer questions or to provide statistics approximately services and products.

9. E-Commerce

ChatGPT can be carried out in e-alternate to reply questions about orders, shipping or returning merchandise. This manner, clients may be supported short and correctly.

Chapter 2: How Can I Use Chatgpt In Exercising?

To use ChatGPT efficaciously, look at those steps.

1. Choose a suitable platform

ChatGPT is available on numerous systems, which incorporates internet apps, cellular apps or messaging systems like WhatsApp or Facebook Messenger. Choose the platform that brilliant fits your needs.

2. Now formulate your questions or request

Think approximately what questions you want to ask ChatGPT. Try to formulate your questions sincerely and precisely so that ChatGPT will apprehend them extra without issues. The greater information you offer ChatGPT in your question, the higher the surrender stop end result of the answer can be.

Practical examples:

Correctly formulated:

"How can I boom my productivity in the domestic place of business?"

"Can you supply me a very good recipe for gluten-free bread?"

"What are the blessings and disadvantages of various CMS systems?"

Incorrectly formulated:

"I want domestic workplace hints."

"Give me a recipe for bread."

"Tell me about CMS structures."

The incorrectly worded questions are too desired and difficult to understand, which may additionally additionally confuse ChatGPT or purpose it not to provide the statistics you need. The correctly worded questions, as an alternative, are easy and specific, at the way to assist ChatGPT offer greater accurate answers that can help you remedy your trouble or accumulate your desires.

three.   Start the verbal exchange

Open the chosen chat platform and start the verbal exchange with ChatGPT. In most times, ChatGPT will robotically greet you and prompt you to ask your questions. For longer dialogs at the equal topic, ChatGPT will pay hobby to the statistics already exchanged earlier in the verbal exchange and keeps to gather on it.

four.   Give feedback

ChatGPT is designed to take a look at and improve from its experience. If you are satisfied with ChatGPT's response, you may provide them remarks to show them that they are doing an excellent hobby. However, in case you aren't glad with the solution, deliver remarks as properly so that ChatGPT can enhance.

5.   Use the consequences

Once you've got had been given the statistics you want, you could use the results to treatment your issues or advantage your desires.   Use   the   statistics   to   make knowledgeable picks or to enhance your paintings or existence.

6. Stay well mannered

Although ChatGPT is a robotic, it is crucial to stay polite and respectful. Avoid insulting ChatGPT or using it in the incorrect way. Remember that ChatGPT is also utilized by others and is an crucial a part of the web network.

By following these steps, you may efficaciously use ChatGPT and take benefit of its powerful synthetic intelligence to your expert dreams.

How do I create enormous texts?

To create substantial textual content with ChatGPT, it's far essential to formulate and set the seed, context, and activates effectively. Here is an evidence of a way to apply those factors efficaciously.

1. Seed

The Seed is used by ChatGPT to begin generating textual content. It is a quick collection of text that serves as a start line for producing text. The seed need to be a short however concise area to begin that presentations the overall direction of the textual content you want to jot down down. For example, your seed is probably "Artificial intelligence is one of the most interesting era of our time" in case you need to put in writing down a piece of writing about AI.

2. Context

Context refers to the data that ChatGPT have to take into account while producing textual content. The context may be something that has an effect at the textual content generator, at the side of records about the scenario, the goal market, the cause of the text, and so forth. To make sure that the generated text is ordinary and applicable, it's far essential to certainly outline the context.

three. Prompts

Prompts are specific commands or questions which may be meant to cause ChatGPT to consist of extremely good data or subjects in the text this is generated. Prompts can be very beneficial to manual text technology and make sure that the generated textual content meets the necessities. For example, a fixed off might be "Describe the benefits of AI for organizations" or "Explain how a neural community works".

You can efficaciously control ChatGPT's text era and generate sizable text that meets requirements and expectancies with the aid of way of the usage of Seed, Context and Prompts correctly.

How can ChatGPT installation and shape a text in an attractive way?

By responding to particular steerage and input, ChatGPT allow you to structure a textual content and create an appealing define. Here are some steps you could follow to have ChatGPT create a primarily based outline for you.

1.   Define the problem and cause of the text you need to put in writing. Think about the principle elements you need to cover and the subtopics or details you need to embody inside the textual content.

2.   Use specific commands "Prompts" to present an define of the problem of the text. State a clean question or challenge consider on which you need to put in writing.

3.   Use "Seed" and "Context" to persuade the model in a specific course and make sure that the textual content is customized to the famous concern don't forget. For example, you could specify key terms, key phrases, or a few key factors to be protected within the text.

four.   After you have got were given made the enter, ChatGPT will generate a response. Review the generated texts and pick the parts you want to encompass for your define. Arrange the text fragments in a logical order and write a quick precis for every section.

five. Use the information you bought from the generated textual content to install writing down your very very very own summary and advent. Make sure the outline is nicely-mounted and logical, with a clean hierarchy of maximum important points and subtopics.

6. Review your outline and textual content cautiously to make sure they may be smooth, understandable, and serve the motive of the textual content.

Overall, when it comes to structuring a textual content and growing an attractive define, ChatGPT may be a precious beneficial useful resource. With the proper input and steering, ChatGPT will can help you installation your thoughts and accelerate the writing method.

What blessings does artificial intelligence

ChatGPT carry me?

It is already beyond doubt that ChatGPT will change or even revolutionize the working worldwide inside the long time. Therefore, you can already enjoy the blessings of synthetic intelligence ChatGPT in diverse fields nowadays.

1. Automation

Artificial intelligence can automate repetitive responsibilities, saving time and power. This lets in remote personnel to consciousness on more complex obligations.

2. Improvement of difficult work first-rate

By the use of synthetic intelligence, responsibilities can be finished quicker and greater exactly, primary to an improvement within the high-quality of labor effects.

three. Flexibility

Artificial intelligence permits the optimization and model of hard work strategies to answer to market modifications and contact for.

four. Cost ordinary overall performance

Artificial intelligence can assist reduce prices for a ways off art work thru way of utilising computerized strategies and selling green artwork strategies.

five. Expanded capabilities

By the use of artificial intelligence, a ways off personnel can increase their skills and knowledge thru having access to assets which include tool analyzing, facts assessment, and incredible generation.

Chapter 3: Use Chatgpt As A Educate On Your Very Personal Paintings

ChatGPT may be used as a teach in your private artwork in numerous tactics.

1. Feedback on written texts

You can use ChatGPT to get comments for your written texts. Give ChatGPT a pattern of your text and permit it suggest a revision. Read the revised text and remarks carefully and use it to decorate your very personal text.

2. Generating mind

If you're having trouble generating new thoughts for a assignment or task, you can use ChatGPT to generate thoughts. Give ChatGPT a topic or query and permit it generate a list of thoughts. Use these thoughts as a place to begin on your private questioning and innovative techniques.

three.   Questions and solutions

ChatGPT moreover can be used as a educate for questions and solutions. If you're having hassle locating a method to a specific question, kind the question into ChatGPT and allow it generate an answer. Review the solution carefully and use it to support your very very own questioning and research.

4. Source of thought

ChatGPT moreover can be used as a deliver of concept. Let ChatGPT generate a random text and take a look at through it. Use the thoughts or terms you need to enhance or expand your very very own tasks or responsibilities.

It is important to phrase that ChatGPT is a device and can't replace all components of a human schooling relationship. Use ChatGPT as a supplement on your very very very own art work and integrate it with human feedback and education to get the amazing effects.

Are there any guidelines on the

use of ChatGPT?

Yes, there are a few guidelines on the usage of ChatGPT that should be taken under consideration.

1. Limited information

Although ChatGPT is able to acting a whole lot of obligations, its solutions are primarily based definitely completely simplest at the statistics it have end up capable of get right of entry to within the route of its training. Thus, if a person asks a query that is out of doors the scope of ChatGPT's education data set, ChatGPT might not be able to offer the first rate solution.

2. Data Quality

The best of the information on which ChatGPT is skilled can have an effect on its capability to provide appropriate responses. If the education statistics is inadequate or faulty, this may purpose terrible outcomes.

three. Abuse

As with each different technology, ChatGPT can be misused. For example, it is able to be used to unfold disinformation or faux facts, or to use beside the factor or offensive language.

four. Privacy Policy

Because ChatGPT accesses statistics and information that customers provide, there can be a possibility that customers' privacy may be violated. It is critical to make certain that the structures on which ChatGPT is used placed into effect enough security functions to protect consumer privateness.

5. Bias

Through the training dataset on which it is primarily based, ChatGPT may additionally moreover inherit subconscious biases. For instance, if the dataset has a bias in the path of a particular organization or culture, this can have an effect on ChatGPT's responses. It is critical to make sure that the training dataset is balanced and freed from bias. This will make certain that ChatGPT responds correctly and quite.

Glossary and clarification of commonplace terms within the vicinity of artificial intelligence

Artificial Intelligence (AI)

Artificial intelligence refers to machines which is probably able to appearing human-like intelligence obligations, along with speech reputation, image reputation, phrase processing, and preference making.

Machine Learning

Machine reading is a technique of AI that uses algorithms to look at from records and make predictions with out being explicitly programmed.

Deep Learning

Deep studying is a complex form of device learning that makes use of layered neural networks to carry out complicated duties like photo recognition and language processing.

Neural community

A neural community is an set of rules stimulated through the use of the way the human mind works and consists of many interconnected neurons.

Chapter 4: Natural Language Processing (Nlp)

Natural language processing refers back to the method of processing human speech thru computer systems, along with speech reputation and speech technology.

Computer Vision

Computer imaginative and prescient refers to the technique of processing pix and video through manner of computer systems, along with photo recognition and object detection.

Reinforcement Learning

Reinforcement reading is a way of device studying wherein an set of guidelines can research thru trial-and-errors thru being rewarded for suitable picks and punished for horrific ones.

Big Data

Big Data refers to big statistics units which are too massive or too complicated to be processed using conventional facts processing methods.

Algorithm

An algorithm is a step-through-step guide for fixing a trouble or performing a challenge thru the use of a laptop.

IoT (Internet of Things)

The Internet of Things refers to the networking of physical gadgets such as sensors, cameras and home home equipment to accumulate and proportion data.

III. Possible applications of ChatGPT at work

In this financial wreck, diverse professions and industries are provided in which ChatGPT can play an crucial feature. By the use of ChatGPT, organizations can automate many repetitive responsibilities, saving time and prices. This lets in for extra time to focus on strategic selections and offer customized customer care.

In addition, severa income possibilities are supplied, which might be specifically appropriate for operating from domestic and might offer a sturdy, passive profits within the long term. These consist of on-line surveys, where you get paid for completing surveys, affiliate advertising and advertising and marketing, in that you earn a charge with the useful resource of the usage of promoting merchandise from specific companies, similarly to textual content and content material fabric creation, wherein you are taking on freelance writing or content cloth advent projects and art work on them from domestic.

Continue analyzing to have a observe extra approximately the software possibilities of ChatGPT in diverse fields.

1. Online surveys

A famous manner to make cash from domestic is through on line surveys. Businesses and agencies regularly want feedback from customers to decorate their products and services and optimize their advertising and advertising strategies. In order to earn money or coupons, you may be a part of up with survey net sites and take surveys on a regular basis.

You need to join up with legitimate survey net websites to earn coins from on-line surveys. Toluna, Swagbucks and GlobalTestMarket are some famous websites. You can fill out your profiles on those web websites to make certain that you simplest acquire surveys that healthful your profile.

Depending at the internet net site and survey, charge for on line surveys varies. Some surveys might also moreover handiest take a few minutes and earn you some cents. Other surveys may also moreover take longer and earn you severa dollars. To maximize your income, it is vital to take surveys frequently.

Although on line surveys are an clean manner to earn cash from domestic, you need to be conscious that there are a few drawbacks. The pay can be highly low, and it is able to be difficult to discover enough surveys to earn a steady earnings. Also, there are various fraudulent websites that promise to offer immoderate bills for surveys, but are absolutely simply out to accumulate your private statistics. Make positive that you use legitimate survey net sites and have a look at the phrases of use cautiously earlier than signing as an awful lot as their net web sites.

Useful internet hyperlinks on the topic of on line surveys:

2. Virtual assistant sports activities sports

As a VA, you can provide administrative, organizational, and technical assist to corporations and people at the equal time as running out of your property. As a VA, you could carry out responsibilities which consist of managing e mail, information entry, scheduling excursion, dealing with social media, accounting, customer support, and further.

There are many on-line structures to discover VA jobs, along side Upwork, Fiverr, and Remote.Co. Of route, you may furthermore take a look at right now to agencies or mother and father which can be in need of VA services and provide your offerings.

You have to have administrative, organizational, and technical talents to attain achievement as a VA. Since you will be interacting with customers and co-employees, you've got with a view to organize and prioritize your paintings correctly and characteristic exceptional verbal exchange talents.

Compensation for VA jobs is depending on the person and complexity of the venture. Some jobs can be paid on an hourly foundation, at the same time as others can also have a flat charge. It's crucial to have easy agreements along with your clients. Make certain you are becoming paid effectively in your artwork.

Virtual assistant jobs are in particular suitable for people with actual administrative abilties and experience, and provide a flexible manner to earn cash from domestic.

Useful net hyperlinks to find out jobs as a digital assistant (VA):

Indeed

Remote.Co

Virtual Assistant Jobs

Freelancer

three. Web layout and development

You are accountable for designing, developing, and programming internet websites and packages as an internet style fashion designer and developer. You can every freelance or work for an internet design or advertising and marketing business enterprise. The gain of freelancing is that you could make money working from home. This offers you greater flexibility.

You need to be expert in client interface layout and programming in diverse languages collectively with HTML, CSS, JavaScript, PHP and further to be successful as a web fashion designer and developer. You may also need to be professional inside the utilization of Content Management Systems like WordPress, Magento or Shopware.

In addition, you need as a manner to design websites which may be in track with the needs of your customers. This consists of keeping up with the cutting-edge design traits and technological inclinations.

You can take on-line courses, webinars, or tutorials to decorate your capabilities as an internet style clothier and developer. There are many structures together with Udemy, Lynda, or Skillshare that provide courses on severa topics which include internet layout, internet development, or consumer enjoy.

You can also locate jobs on structures like Upwork, Freelancer, or Fiverr.

Another preference is to market your offerings right away to customers thru developing your non-public internet website and supplementing it with advertising on social media net websites which incorporates Facebook and Instagram.

Web layout and development initiatives may be paid on a flat rate basis or with the useful resource of the hour. Compensation is predicated upon on the sort and scope of the task, as well as your enjoy and skills.

Overall, running as a web dressmaker and developer is a superb way to earn a living from home and use your skills in a fast-paced and exciting enterprise. However, it calls for an entire lot of hobby and determination to achieve fulfillment and keep customers glad.

Useful net links that permit you to studies extra approximately net layout and improvement and deepen your expertise:

An interactive on-line reading platform that gives loose guides in HTML, CSS, JavaScript and distinct programming languages.

An on-line platform for e-analyzing courses wherein you may discover numerous courses on internet layout, net improvement and different subjects.

A loose online internet development aid that offers tutorials and reference fabric on HTML, CSS, JavaScript, and awesome net technology.

A net web site with tutorials, code snippets and assets on CSS.

An on line platform supplying articles and tutorials on internet format and development.

An on line platform for internet developers and architects with articles, tutorials and courses on numerous topics related to web improvement.

Smashing Magazine –

An on-line magazine for internet designers and builders that competencies articles and tutorials on severa topics which encompass UX layout, net improvement and the the front-surrender techniques.

4. Copywriting and Content Creation

Copywriting and content cloth creation are special methods to make cash from home. If you experience writing and have a revolutionary streak, you could use your skills to create replica and content material for corporations and internet internet websites.

Here are steps you could take to put together for a career in copywriting and content fabric introduction.

Improve your writing talents

If you want to come to be a top notch creator, you need to enhance your writing skills. Read books, articles, and blogs to make yourself familiar with one of a kind writing styles and techniques.

Choose your vicinity of hobby

There are many varieties of content material you could create, from blog posts to social media posts to product descriptions and e-books. Think about what form of content fabric you can pleasant create and what problem do not forget pursuits you.

Create a portfolio net website on line

To persuade capability clients, you need to create a portfolio internet site wherein you may show off your satisfactory paintings. Here you can moreover embody your touch records and pricing statistics.

Network

Use social media and professional networks like LinkedIn to connect to awesome writers and capacity clients. You can also take part in on-line forums and writing companies to get feedback and help.

Work on your advertising and marketing

To entice customers, you need to market your services. Create a advertising and marketing package with a charge list and examples of your work and ship it to capability clients.

More recommendations for a achievement copywriting and content material material creation:

Write clean and concise duplicate that speaks to the wishes of your target marketplace.

Pay hobby to spelling and grammar.

Adhere to the consumer's specifications regarding the fashion and tone of the texts.

Stay up to date on content fabric tendencies and super practices.

There are many net web sites alongside side Textbroker, Content.De or perhaps Upwork in which you can discover jobs as a copywriter or content fabric fabric creator. If you think about a specific place of hobby, you can moreover look for corporations that need content material cloth in that place of interest.

five. Translation and enhancing

A excessive stage of fluency in as a minimum languages is wanted to work as a domestic translator or proofreader. As a contemporary rule, to art work as a translator or proofreader, you must be fluent in one of the overseas languages and function a fantastic command of your neighborhood language.

Good know-how of grammar, spelling, syntax, and punctuation is important. If you determine as a translator, you want to additionally be able to translate the fashion, nuance and that means of the precise text into the goal language.

Another crucial element is that, as a translator or proofreader, you want to be dependable and deliver the art work in your clients on time. Meeting final dates is essential to earning the consider of your clients and constructing an top notch recognition.

To art work efficiently as a home translator or proofreader, you can take specialized guides or certificate to beautify your language skills and display your competencies. You also can find jobs that healthy your abilities and revel in on many on-line mission boards and structures.

Establishing yourself inside the market and building a remarkable reputation is an important part of being a a fulfillment paintings-from-home translator or proofreader.

This may be finished via excessive fine paintings, properly time manage and verbal exchange together with your customers.

6. Social Media Management

Another popular opportunity to make cash from domestic is social media manage. Essentially, this refers to handling a agency's or person's social media presence. This includes content material cloth introduction, positioned up scheduling, remark management, and social media channel widespread average performance evaluation.

Depending at the customer, the necessities for social media control jobs can range substantially. Some possible requirements can also encompass:

Proficiency in diverse social media structures which include Facebook, Twitter, Instagram, TikTok and LinkedIn.

Ability to create attractive and innovative content material material

Experience in growing social media strategies

Understanding of social media analytics equipment to measure the success of campaigns

Customer hobby and potential to speak efficiently with customers or customers

Social media manipulate may be a useful commercial employer, as many companies have found out how essential a strong social media presence is to their fulfillment. If you've got the vital skills, you can look for social media control jobs via on-line manner boards or social media corporations.

Useful internet links that allow you to search for social media manipulate jobs:

It additionally may be beneficial to look relevant social media businesses or forums and ask about jobs or possibilities.

7. E-exchange and on line profits

Another amazing manner to make money from home is thru e-exchange and on-line income. There are many possibilities to promote merchandise online and run your very very own online maintain with the growing reputation of on-line shopping, specially after the Corona Pandemic.

There are several systems that make it quite easy to create your personal on line save if you are interested in doing so. These consist of net sites like Shopify, Wix, and

Squarespace. These structures provide templates and equipment for growing expert-looking internet websites and promoting merchandise online.

Alternatively, you can sell merchandise on on line marketplaces like Amazon, eBay, Yatego, or Etsy. These systems can help you promote your merchandise to a far wider goal market and feature systems in location to system orders and payments. As your on-line industrial business enterprise grows and your sales increase, you can moreover want to consider buy processing software software to help you manipulate your enterprise extra professionally. There are companies along facet JTL or Dreamrobot.

If you do no longer need to promote your non-public products, you may moreover paintings as an accomplice marketer and sell specific organizations' products. You earn a fee at the same time as a person buys a product based totally on your advice.

To obtain achievement in e-trade, you need understanding within the following areas:

Product pics and outline

Knowledge of search engine optimization (Search Engine Optimization) and on line advertising and advertising and marketing

Experience in customer support and communique

Knowledge of dealing with online payments and delivery

Basic crook facts may be a bonus

There are many online property that let you installation a web store or promote products in on line marketplaces. Some famous net web sites are:

With a hint effort and time, you may increase your on line save proper right into a a fulfillment and worthwhile industrial agency.

Here is a small choice of the most vital marketplaces in which you could begin your on line enterprise:

8. Affiliate advertising

Affiliate Marketing is a way to make coins on line by using using selling first-rate businesses' services or products and earning commissions for each a achievement sale or lead generated.

There are three crucial occasions in affiliate marketing: the service provider (moreover referred to as the advertiser), the author (furthermore called the partner), and the consumer. The provider issuer offers the products or services, the writer promotes the products or services, and the patron is the simplest who will ultimately purchase or use the products or offerings.

A writer can promote a carrier company's products or services in several procedures. One way is to vicinity an associate link or banner on your internet internet site. When a customer clicks on the link or banner and purchases the goods or offerings or takes a specific movement, the author receives a fee.

Another alternative is electronic mail advertising. The writer can collect an e mail list and send emails to its subscribers to promote the merchant's products or services. When a customer purchases merchandise or takes a selected movement primarily based totally on those emails, the publisher gets a fee.

One of the most important benefits of affiliate advertising and advertising and marketing is that it receives rid of the need which will make bigger your very private services or products, allowing you to truly promote the goods or offerings of numerous organizations in exchange for reimbursement for a achievement profits or lead technology. There are hundreds of companion networks that be a part of publishers with traders and control the processing of commissions.

It is essential to discover a area of interest that you apprehend and in which you've got a committed goal market that allows you to reap fulfillment in associate marketing. It is also essential to pick out services or products that wholesome this area of interest and are of excessive tremendous. The author need to also make sure that he or she has sufficient traffic on his or her internet website on-line or email list to generate sufficient clicks on his or her affiliate links or banners.

Overall, companion advertising can be a worthwhile manner to make cash on line. If you find out the proper area of interest and popularity on excessive splendid products or services. However, it moreover requires a superb amount of hard work and staying strength to achieve success.

9. Creative writing and e-book authorship

Creative writing and e-book authorship also are extraordinary techniques to make cash from home. If you adore to put in writing and feature a passion for literature, this interest will let you apprehend your dream of a profession as a author and earn coins at the same time.

You can make money working from home and create your private stories, novels, poems and fantastic literary works as a innovative writer or book writer. You can self-post your artwork or have it posted thru using a author to bring it to a much broader target audience. There are many techniques to marketplace your paintings, which consist of social media, readings and signings, and writing contests.

Writing and operating in the direction of regularly, similarly to editing and refining your paintings to ensure it is of excessive super, is crucial to being a a success e book writer. It also may be beneficial to discover a community of like-minded human beings to provide manual and remarks.

There are incredible techniques to apply your writing capabilities to make coins from home. These embody ghostwriting, improving, and proofreading. As a ghostwriter, you could write for others who may not have the time or abilities to put in writing down themselves.

Editing and proofreading are also important offerings for writers, as they may help to ensure that your artwork is free of errors and that it is nicely written.

It can be very thrilling and interesting to make cash from home as a creative author or e-book author. However, it additionally takes some of strength of mind and exercising to acquire achievement.

10. Podcasting and YouTube

Podcasts and YouTube movies are topics you have got in all likelihood heard of. They're well-known media codecs. They're often used for enjoyment or facts. But podcasts and YouTube can also be used to make cash from domestic.

Podcasts are recorded audio or video that can be accessed on-line. These recordings can be created on numerous subjects at the side of politics, sports activities, manner of life or commercial agency. There are many a achievement podcasts that have a huge target market, which makes them attractive to advertisers. So, when you have a passion for a nice problem rely and revel in talking or doing interviews, podcasting can be an exciting possibility for you.

YouTube offers similar opportunities to podcasting, but within the shape of video content material. There are countless YouTubers who are very a achievement and characteristic tens of hundreds of thousands of subscribers. These are frequently splendor, gaming, comedy or academic films on precise topics. Again, advertising and advertising and marketing and marketing is an vital supply of profits for YouTubers. So YouTube could be an thrilling choice for you if you enjoy being inside the front of the virtual digicam, have innovative mind and some abilities in video manufacturing.

To gain success in this project, it is crucial to assemble a committed following.

This technique: You have to usually create awesome content material fabric that engages your audience. It's additionally critical to find out a smooth area of interest and give attention to a selected situation be counted to attraction to a target market.

With podcasting and YouTube, there are various awesome methods to make cash. Advertising is one of the maximum popular strategies to make coins. If you have got an entire lot of visitors or listeners, advertisers may additionally additionally take word and pay you to location their commercials to your films. Sponsorship is also an opportunity, wherein you receives a rate to say or characteristic a specific product or brand. You also can offer your personal products or services related to your concern count, together with products or on line publications.

Chapter 5: Online Instruct And Consultant

As an internet educate or representative, you have have been given the opportunity to provide your understanding or experience in a specific region to first-rate people and help them acquire their desires. You can provide your education or consulting thru numerous structures in conjunction with Skype, Zoom or similar gadget, permitting you to paintings from the comfort of your private home.

To achieve fulfillment as an internet train or consultant, you must have records and enjoy for your discipline, similarly to a great understanding of your clients' wishes. Good time control and powerful communication skills are also critical to your achievement as an internet train or consultant.

Possible industries for on-line education or consulting:

Career counseling

Personality improvement

Financial making plans and consulting

Fitness and health

Relationship counseling

There are severa systems and internet websites wherein you could offer your training or consulting offerings, which consist of Coach.Me, BetterHelp, or Clarity.Fm.

It is likewise possible to offer your offerings in your very private net web site and promote them through targeted advertising and marketing.

As a web train or consultant, you can provide your offerings on an hourly or flat price basis. The rate frequently is predicated upon for your understanding and revel in, as well as the call for for your unique area.

Photography and image layout

It is turning into an increasing number of well-known to earn money as a photographer or photograph designer from home. Businesses and people are more and more looking for expert pics and pictures to beautify their on line presence as social media and on-line advertising and advertising end up extra important.

As a chunk-from-domestic photographer, you could produce stock pictures for inventory photo companies or receive commissions from customers who're in want of pix, wedding ceremony pictures or product shots. To reap success in this issue, you will need proper device further to understanding of photo enhancing.

As a homebased picture designer, you can have the opportunity to address masses of obligations. These include developing emblems, flyers, brochures, banners, and extra. Knowledge of photo format device together with Adobe Photoshop, Illustrator or InDesign is a plus. Creativity and an eye fixed constant for aesthetics are also a plus.

Both of these alternatives offer a excessive degree of flexibility and the functionality to earn a living from home and to deliver your very very own responsibilities to existence.

However, it is crucial to have a top notch understanding of a manner to market your very very very own artwork and to have a community of contacts if you want to reach capability customers.

Also, with such a lot of humans providing their services, there is lots of competition in those regions. To stand proud of the competition, it is truely useful to hobby on a particular niche marketplace and recognition on a specific region.

Overall, a honestly exciting way to be innovative and make coins at the identical time is through domestic-based pics and photograph layout possibilities. This might be the way to move if you have a passion for visual aesthetics and revel in expressing your self creatively.

App improvement and programming

Another choice for a a success home commercial enterprise is app improvement and programming. With the growing reputation of smartphones and capsules, the call for for apps for diverse features is also developing.

You commonly need an great information of programming languages like Java, Swift, PHP or Python to end up an app developer or programmer. However, there are also gear like App Builder that will let you create easy apps whilst now not having to recognize the way to code.

From growing cellular video video video games to developing productivity apps to programming advanced net applications, working as an app developer may be very numerous.

Looking for mission art work on freelance systems like Upwork, Freelancer.De or Fiverr is one way to work at home as an app developer. Here, builders can look for jobs that during shape their talents and hobbies and communicate with clients to make clear their requirements and complete their artwork.

Creating your very own apps and selling them on the App Store or Google Play Store is some other manner to paintings as a home-based truly app developer. However, this requires not quality programming abilities, however moreover statistics of advertising and profits.

An important trouble for fulfillment as an app developer is the capacity to constantly make bigger and maintain up with the present day day era and traits in the employer. This moreover consists of the willingness to teach oneself and frequently attend trainings and guides.

In precis, going for walks as an app developer is a hard and profitable possibility, but one which calls for in-intensity know-how of programming and era, similarly to fantastic commercial enterprise talents.

Codecademy, Udacity, Coursera, and edX provide on line courses that train the basics of programming and app development, assisting you benefit the talents and know-how you need. These guides variety from newbie guides to superior subjects like system studying and synthetic intelligence.

GitHub is a web-primarily based in reality version manage device used by builders to control and share their initiatives. It's an crucial part of the development approach and a remarkable aid for taking part with special developers.

Online marketplace studies

Online market studies is the gathering and assessment of information to manual advertising alternatives. Online research can take numerous forms, which encompass surveys, consciousness businesses, and observational research. Companies lease research agencies to build up statistics to help them enhance their services and products or increase new services and products.

Survey individuals in a web studies take a look at may be paid for answering severa questions or taking component in recognition agencies or observational research. Payment is frequently primarily based mostly on how an awful lot effort and time the player locations into the have a look at. There also are a few net web web sites that allow customers to earn elements that can be redeemed for coins or gift playing playing cards through way of finishing on-line surveys or taking detail in other sorts of studies sports activities activities.

If you want to take part in on-line marketplace studies, there are many real internet web sites and market studies businesses that provide such opportunities. However, you ought to be cautious when deciding on a net website because there are various scams in which people promise to earn pretty some cash however in the long run they do now not gets a commission the least bit.

It is vital to take a look at the phrases and conditions and extraordinary users' opinions before signing up for a web market research net site.

Overall, taking part in on-line market research may be an clean and flexible manner to earn cash from domestic. It does no longer require any specific competencies or experience, surely your very very very own opinion and some time.

Data Entry and Data Acquisition

Data get admission to and records capture are vital sports for businesses, companies, and exclusive entities. They include the collection, verification, and manipulation of statistics in digital form. Data access regularly includes much less difficult duties which include transcribing statistics, while facts seize includes greater complicated processes that contain merging and preparing information from a couple of assets.

Data get right of entry to and data seize sports activities might also additionally include, for example, moving into addresses, verifying information for accuracy, entering statistics into databases, and merging information from certainly one of a type assets. It is an hobby often used to behavior surveys, marketplace studies, and consumer interviews.

It can frequently make enjoy for corporations to outsource the ones obligations to maintain time and assets. This allows employees to popularity at the organisation's center business on the equal time as records processing is outsourced.

The necessities for jogging in facts entry and records capture variety depending on the customer and the nature of the interest. In tremendous, but, rapid typing competencies and a excessive degree of interest are a bonus. Familiarity with diverse statistics processing packages and databases is likewise essential.

One manner to get worried in this area is to look for online jobs or work with groups that specialize in this form of issuer. There are also structures that join freelancers with corporations that need records access services.

In summary, Data Entry and Data Entry are vital sports activities sports which may be needed in lots of companies. It is an preference for humans who've proper writing skills, immoderate cognizance degree and would love to artwork in the region of information processing.

Chapter 6: Transcription And Audio Text Creation

Transcription and audio textual content creation is any other opportunity for working on-line. It refers back to the conversion of audio or video documents into textual content documents. This art work is appropriate for people with right listening abilities and speedy writing tempo.

Transcription paintings can be carried out for some of customers which embody companies, studies institutions, media corporations, academic establishments, and loads of others. Transcriptions can come from interviews, meetings, meetings, dictations, podcasts, lectures, and lots of different kinds of audio or video recordings.

There are styles of transcription duties, verbatim and non-verbatim. Verbatim transcriptions seize all the phrases and utterances spoken inside the audio recording, which incorporates history noise, laughter and pauses. Non-verbatim transcriptions embody nice the most vital information spoken within the audio recording.

Transcription generally requires a computer, a headset, and transcription software program program. There are many loose and paid transcription device that may be used to make the task easier. Tasks are normally paid consistent with minute of audio (PMA) or in line with hour of exertions (PHA).

Compensation is typically primarily based totally on the trouble of the audio material and the quantity of the transcription. In addition to transcription, on-line audio copywriters can also provide services collectively with subtitling, translation, and audio translation.

For folks that revel in running on my own and are obsessed on audio and voice recording, transcription and audio copywriting can be an incredible in shape. Good articulation, rapid typing, and tremendous spelling and grammar are important for this work.

It is crucial to observe that this artwork calls for time and persistence, as it's miles frequently vital to delve into the audio material and make many corrections so as to produce an extensive text.

There are many unique structures that offer comparable services. However, it's far essential to cautiously maintain in thoughts which platform super fits your goals.

Technical help and helpdesk

Technical useful resource and help desk are responsibilities that require information and technical expertise to help customers with technical problems and offer answers. Support may be provided with the resource of phone, e mail, or far off get admission to to the purchaser's pc.

A help table employee ought with the intention to solution technical questions from clients and manual them via feasible solutions. This can include troubles with hardware, software, or network connectivity.

It is likewise vital to have notable interpersonal skills. This guarantees that the customer is well looked after at every diploma of the useful resource system.

Tech guide and help desk artwork can be a incredible way to make money working from home, as many companies provide far off art work and flexible hours. Skills and qualifications required can range relying on the corporation. However, enjoy in the IT or technical assist industry is regularly critical.

A technical help or assist table expert might also moreover additionally art work as a representative, helping corporations enhance their IT systems and strategies. This concern can also contain developing education and academic substances to help customers decorate their technical abilities.

In precis, technical resource and help table is a notable manner to help clients with technical troubles and assist companies optimize their IT systems.

Online education and e-gaining knowledge of

Online schooling and e-studying is a wonderful manner to replace facts and abilities on line. More and further humans are taking benefit of this sort of schooling to boom their careers, examine new capabilities, or in reality maintain their schooling for personal use.

Online education can are available a number of codecs. These include video classes, live webinars, interactive guides, and extra. Courses can be unfastened or paid, relying on the provider and content material.

Online training is available in lots of areas, in conjunction with languages, programming, digital advertising and marketing and advertising, layout, cooking, fitness, and masses of others. There are numerous structures wherein you can discover such publications, and a whole lot of them provide certificate or ranges to boom the charge to the participant.

Flexibility and the functionality to get right of access to publications each time, anywhere are the benefits of on line training and e-getting to know. They also are often much less highly-priced than conventional training formats and provide the functionality to awareness on specific topics.

For agencies, e-gaining knowledge of systems also offer the possibility to teach employees and make sure that they will be constantly updated.

Game trying out and evaluation

One manner to make coins on line is to check and overview video games. Game testing is the approach of checking the content material material, capabilities, pictures, and specific factors of video video games to make sure that they run smoothly and provide a fun and interesting enjoy. This is an crucial step in sport development, as insects and errors want to be placed in advance than the sport is released.

There are severa styles of video video games that may be tested, which includes console, PC, and cell video video video games. To make sure that they test all components of the sport, testers are typically given a guide or tick list to observe. The results are then shared with the developer or publisher to repair problems and decorate the gaming experience.

As a game tester, you can both be hired straight away by using way of way of the developer or you will be hired thru a specialised finding out employer. Pay can variety relying on the organisation and the form of labor, however is usually amongst 10 and 20 Euros in line with hour. Some companies furthermore provide bonuses or distinct perks which incorporates free video video games or hardware.

In addition to trying out video video games, you can additionally earn cash with the resource of reviewing video video games. In this case, you will be asked to provide your opinion approximately a recreation with the resource of gambling it and writing a examine. These ratings are used by activity developers and publishers to get remarks from gamers and beautify the game enjoy.

Overall, video game sorting out and rating is a amusing hobby to make coins online, in particular for those who have a passion for video video games. It requires staying power, hobby to information and the capability to formulate remarks constructively.

Customer provider and assist

The capability to offer customer service and assistance is crucial for lots corporations to offer the excellent possible carrier and assist to their clients. With the growing variety of online clients, the want for immediate and effective customer service has emerge as critical for corporations.

Online customer support and guide involves an entire lot of duties, which includes answering client inquiries through e mail, chat, or phone; managing orders and courtroom instances; acting technical assist obligations; and supplying education and tutorials to clients. Good customer service can collect consumer believe and loyalty, that could motive business organisation growth and achievement.

Working in customer service and assist generally requires a strong customer interest, brief wondering, suitable conversation abilities, the ability to paintings in a hard and fast, and a tremendous mind-set. Experience the usage of patron relationship control (CRM) systems and one-of-a-type assist equipment also can be an advantage.

There are numerous methods to artwork in online customer support and help. For instance, you may paintings for a business company as a customer service consultant or art work independently as a digital assistant for numerous clients. Starting your very non-public online useful resource enterprise business employer is another manner to paintings in this hassle.

Overall, jogging in customer support and assist gives nicely alternatives to earn a living from home even as improving customer service and pleasure.

IV. ChatGPT – Time Management and Work-Life Balance

Improve time manipulate with ChatGPT

Effective time and aid management is essential for the achievement of any business. ChatGPT can help enhance time manage within the place of job with the aid of using automating duties and optimizing strategies.

Automation of recurring responsibilities

ChatGPT can help automate ordinary obligations with the resource of mechanically managing repetitive duties. For instance, ChatGPT can assist in answering emails, scheduling appointments, or generating critiques. By automating the ones duties, time may be saved and allotted to extra vital and disturbing obligations.

Optimization of tough paintings strategies

ChatGPT can also assist streamline paintings procedures via supporting to plan and prepare duties and obligations. For instance, ChatGPT can assist create schedules and assign obligations to make sure that all duties are finished on time. ChatGPT also can assist display screen and update the development of initiatives to ensure that the entirety is on foot without problems.

Better collaboration

Collaboration and verbal exchange internal a group may be more potent through using ChatGPT. For instance, team contributors can make use of ChatGPT to speak speedy and successfully, minimizing misunderstandings. ChatGPT can also assist in coordinating obligations and initiatives, making sure that each one stakeholders are on the identical net net web page.

ChatGPT and scheduling

ChatGPT also can help in time and aid planning by way of imparting help in developing schedules and time manipulate strategies. It can assist prioritize duties and allocate time buffers to account for unexpected activities and delays. ChatGPT can also aid in monitoring and reading time usage to apprehend weaknesses and optimize strategies.

ChatGPT and strength of mind

ChatGPT can help in improving strength of will via helping task prioritization and time and useful useful resource management. For example, it can assist create to-do lists and schedules to make sure all responsibilities are finished. ChatGPT can also aid in enhancing recognition and focus on essential responsibilities by using assisting in minimizing distractions and interruptions.

ChatGPT and challenge manage

An development in undertaking manage can be completed through the assist of ChatGPT in making plans, organizing, and monitoring responsibilities. For instance, ChatGPT can help create schedules and assign duties to make sure the well timed of entirety of all assignments. It can also assist in tracking and updating challenge development to make certain easy operations. Additionally, ChatGPT can enhance communique among severa mission stakeholders and make sure every body is on the identical web page.

ChatGPT and stress discount

Another manner ChatGPT can help with time manage is thru reducing stress. By automating recurring responsibilities and optimizing paintings techniques, ChatGPT can assist reduce workload and therefore lower stress stages for employees. ChatGPT also can useful resource in putting priorities and developing schedules to make sure that each one obligations can be finished in the given cut-off dates.

ChatGPT and flexibility

ChatGPT can help create flexibility in time manipulate. By assisting within the planning and organization of obligations and initiatives, personnel can allocate their time and sources more correctly and flexibly. ChatGPT also can assist alter priorities and schedules in line with converting requirements and dreams, ensuring that all obligations can be finished inside the given cut-off dates.

ChatGPT and time usage analysis

Lastly, ChatGPT also can assist in studying time usage to pick out out weaknesses and optimize techniques. ChatGPT can help measure and examine the time spent on unique obligations and obligations to determine regions wherein upgrades may be made. ChatGPT also can beneficial useful resource in identifying developments and patterns in time usage to optimize the planning and agency of duties and initiatives.

Bottom line

Overall, artificial intelligence ChatGPT can play an important characteristic in expert time manipulate with the useful resource of assisting inside the automation of normal responsibilities, optimizing artwork methods, enhancing teamwork and communique, planning time and property, enhancing electricity of will, helping task manipulate, decreasing strain, fostering flexibility, and reading time usage.

A real art work-existence stability with ChatGPT

Achieving a notable paintings-lifestyles stability is vital for leading a fulfilling lifestyles and being a fulfillment in a single's career. ChatGPT can assist in attaining a better paintings-life balance with the resource of automating repetitive obligations and growing extra time for critical obligations and amusement sports.

Automation of repetitive duties

By automating repetitive tasks, ChatGPT can help hold time that can be allotted to more critical responsibilities or amusement sports. For example, ChatGPT can help in answering emails, developing documents, or studying facts. By automating these duties, the workload may be reduced, allowing greater time for leisure activities and own family.

Better planning and commercial enterprise business enterprise

ChatGPT can assist benefit higher planning and business enterprise of responsibilities and duties. By helping in challenge prioritization and scheduling, ChatGPT can contribute to undertaking a higher artwork-life stability. Employees can better installation their duties and set priorities with the assist of ChatGPT to make certain they'll be in a role to finish their responsibilities on time at the equal time as but having sufficient time for enjoyment sports.

Improved performance

By automating duties and improving making plans and corporation, ChatGPT can contribute to personnel operating extra effectively. This reduces the time desired to finish duties and leaves more time for entertainment sports activities. Improved normal performance can also reduce place of job strain, certainly impacting paintings-lifestyles stability.

Chapter 7: Flexibility And Mobility

ChatGPT can also contribute to sporting out a higher paintings-lifestyles stability by using way of permitting employees to have greater flexibility and mobility. With the ability to get proper of access to applications from everywhere, personnel can adapt their paintings to their personal needs and commitments more effectively. This can assist remodel artwork from being perceived as a burden to an possibility for major a satisfying lifestyles.

Bottom line

ChatGPT can make contributions to accomplishing a better paintings-existence stability by using manner of automating repetitive responsibilities, allowing better making plans and commercial enterprise business enterprise, enhancing efficiency, and offering more flexibility and mobility. As a result, personnel could have more time for important responsibilities and amusement sports activities, fundamental to a extra fascinating existence.

V. Privacy and ethics

in managing ChatGPT

In a worldwide wherein increasingly statistics is being collected and analyzed, companies and clients should take facts safety substantially and adhere to moral requirements. ChatGPT is not any exception and requires particular hobby to make sure that touchy information isn't always misused.

Privacy at the same time as handling ChatGPT

ChatGPT is primarily based on artificial intelligence and system studying, gathering and processing a huge amount of facts. It is essential that the usage of ChatGPT complies with facts protection guidelines and that each one non-public information is dealt with securely and confidentially.

An essential defensive diploma whilst the use of ChatGPT is records encryption. Most

ChatGPT systems make use of SSL (Secure Socket Layer) and TLS (Transport Layer Security) protocols to ensure that all information transmissions are constant and encrypted. Additionally, companies must make sure that they handiest gather records this is vital for the meant cause and that they use this records only for its intended reason.

It is likewise important to inform clients approximately what data is being collected and the manner it is used. Companies should provide smooth and understandable privateness policies and tell clients about how they are able to shield their information.

Ethics in the use of ChatGPT

In addition to records protection, adhering to ethical requirements in managing ChatGPT is of vital importance. ChatGPT has the capability to interpret and make use of statistics in approaches that can enhance ethical issues. Therefore organizations and clients want to ensure that ChatGPT upholds ethical necessities and does no longer reason discrimination or privateness violations.

An essential ethical query in handling ChatGPT issues the use of statistics. Companies need to make certain that they handiest accumulate facts that is crucial for the supposed reason and that those data are dealt with securely and confidentially. The use of records have to be obvious, and customers want to be knowledgeable approximately how their data is being used.

Another moral detail in handling ChatGPT worries using chatbots in customer service. Companies want to make sure that chatbots do not make fake or misleading statements and they understand the privateness of customers. It is likewise vital for clients to have the choice to talk with a real employee in the event that they want to carry out that.

Another ethical question troubles the use of ChatGPT inside the hiring method. Companies should make sure that ChatGPT is used pretty and objectively in the path of the software program segment and that no discriminatory criteria are employed. It is likewise crucial that applicants are evaluated based on their suitability for the location and not excluded due to biases or discrimination.

Another aspect of coping with ChatGPT concerns using language and content fabric. Since ChatGPT is knowledgeable on big datasets, there may be a chance that the set of policies learns and reproduces biases and discriminations in its responses. This can result in exquisite agencies of humans being discriminated in opposition to based totally on gender, ethnicity, or wonderful elements. To cope with this difficulty, agencies need to make sure that their chatbots are regularly checked for biases and discriminations and modified if important.

Privacy

Another essential aspect in coping with ChatGPT is information privateness. Since ChatGPT can method sensitive facts which encompass names, e-mail addresses, telephone numbers, and one-of-a-kind non-public information, companies need to make sure that this information is dealt with securely and confidentially. Companies ought to make certain that each one statistics collected with the useful aid of ChatGPT is handled with the resource of accordance with applicable statistics protection criminal recommendations and policies.

One manner to ensure facts privacy at the identical time as using ChatGPT is to make sure that all records processed with the useful resource of ChatGPT is encrypted and securely saved. Companies need to additionally make sure that simplest legal human beings have get proper of entry to to the data and that every one personnel who have get right of access to to the records are successfully informed and sensitized.

Another critical factor of statistics privacy even as the usage of ChatGPT relates to transparency and manipulate over the amassed data. Companies must make certain that they tell their customers approximately what records is gathered with the useful aid of ChatGPT, how this data is used, and what rights clients need to control and delete their records.

Bottom line

ChatGPT offers many benefits in professional life, however it is also essential to ensure that its utilization is moral and compliant with records safety rules. Companies should make certain that their chatbots are checked for biases and discriminations and that the accrued information is handled securely and confidentially. By thinking about the ones elements, ChatGPT can assist optimize techniques, keep time and assets, and collect a better paintings-lifestyles balance.

VI. Future Prospects of ChatGPT

ChatGPT has already made its way into many organizations and is predicted to play an increasingly more substantial function inside the workplace within the coming years. Here are some of the future opportunities of ChatGPT within the professional sphere.

1. Personalized consumer communication

ChatGPT is anticipated to play a excellent more huge function in customized consumer verbal exchange inside the destiny. By analyzing client information and conduct, ChatGPT can create custom designed messages and offers, thereby growing patron pleasure.

2. Automated strategies

ChatGPT will even play an critical function in system automation. By automating repetitive duties, employees can shop treasured time that can be used for extra demanding responsibilities. ChatGPT will assist make processes even extra inexperienced and optimize them.

3. Better cooperation

ChatGPT will improve collaboration and communication inside businesses. By optimizing paintings strategies and better-coordinating responsibilities and initiatives, ChatGPT will help growth the productiveness and effectiveness of businesses.

four. Support for choice-making

ChatGPT will clearly play an vital function in preference resource as properly. By analyzing information and generating forecasts and predictions, ChatGPT can assist make knowledgeable options and minimize risks.

five. Extended style of competencies

In the future, ChatGPT is anticipated to be organized with an extended sort of functionalities. Through the integration of speech and photograph reputation technology, ChatGPT may be able to automate and optimize complicated duties and strategies. The integration of artificial intelligence and tool studying may also make ChatGPT even more powerful.

6. Multilingualism

In the future, ChatGPT might be even better capable of communicate and paintings in specific languages. This will help improve collaboration in international companies and facilitate conversation with worldwide customers.

7. Improved information protection and ethics

ChatGPT is predicted to have advanced data safety and moral standards within the destiny. Companies can be obligated to make certain that sensitive records isn't misused and that using ChatGPT is in compliance with relevant records protection and moral requirements.

eight. Further development of the era

The era of ChatGPT will hold to comply inside the destiny. New algorithms and generation will make ChatGPT even more effective and versatile. The integration of latest information sources and formats will permit ChatGPT to automate and optimize even greater complicated obligations and processes.

Bottom line

ChatGPT is anticipated to keep gambling a good sized function in expert lifestyles inside the destiny. The advancing development of Artificial Intelligence and NLP era will allow chatbots like ChatGPT to interact in extra human-like conversations and cope with complex responsibilities more efficiently.

The benefits of ChatGPT in the place of job are diverse, beginning from automating regular duties and optimizing artwork strategies to improving collaboration and communication inside groups. ChatGPT also can assist in time and resource planning, further to electricity of will and mission manipulate.

Of course, there also are demanding situations and ability risks related to the usage of chatbots like ChatGPT within the place of job. These encompass information protection and moral concerns, in addition to issues approximately procedure safety and the bogus of human labour via the use of AI-primarily based definitely structures.

Overall, ChatGPT gives wonderful capacity for companies and professionals. It can help growth place of job efficiency and productivity, enhance art work-life balance, and cope with the demanding situations of the modern-day paintings surroundings. Companies that integrate ChatGPT into their workflow will benefit an extended-term aggressive gain and be capable of respond quicker to adjustments and tendencies.

However, the use of ChatGPT and similar generation have to be achieved responsibly and ethically. Companies ought to ensure that sensitive statistics and facts are blanketed and that the deployment of AI-based systems does not purpose useless possibility of human humans.

Chapter 8: What Is A Prompt?

A activate is a essential factor of AI tools like ChatGPT, because it serves because of the fact the enter that triggers the device's language era capabilities. A activate may be a single word, a quick phrase, or a fixed of key phrases that help the device apprehend what you are seeking out.

It's vital to carefully recall the way you phrase your activates whilst the use of AI gadget like ChatGPT. The way you phrase your enter proper now impacts the pleasant and accuracy of the device's response. To get the maximum out of ChatGPT, it is critical to apply smooth and concise prompts that as it must be bring the data you're looking for.

Additionally, you can use precise key phrases and phrases to assist the tool apprehend the context and tone of your request. For instance, the usage of the phrases "assist" or "assist" on your spark off can sign to the tool which you're seeking out guide or steering, on the equal time as using more conversational terms like "inform me approximately" can suggest that you're looking for records.

How to formulate a outstanding set off for ChatGPT

When crafting activates for ChatGPT, it is important to keep in mind severa key elements to ensure the tool generates accurate and beneficial responses. Here's a greater improved model of the factors you said:

1. Clarity and precision: Make fantastic your activates are clean to apprehend and free of extraneous information. Use brief, concise sentences that actually convey your motive. This will assist ChatGPT fast understand what you're asking and generate a applicable response.

2. Context and specificity: Be unique and provide context even as asking questions. This will supply ChatGPT a better know-how of what you are seeking out and bring about more significant responses.

three. Word preference: The phrases you use in your turns on can drastically impact ChatGPT's know-how of your request. Use easy, common terms and avoid jargon, slang, or overly technical phrases that could confuse the device.

4. Avoiding yes/no or enormous questions: Avoid asking questions that may be replied with a easy advantageous or no, in addition to overly elegant questions which may be hard to reply. Instead, ask unique and nicely-defined questions a terrific manner to allow ChatGPT to generate greater useful responses.

five. Final assessment: Before sending your activate to ChatGPT, take a second to reread and make certain it as it should be conveys your reason and context. This will help ChatGPT understand the context and generate higher responses.

By following those recommendations, you can create powerful and informative activates so one can result in incredible responses from ChatGPT.

Examples of real and terrible turns on

When the use of ChatGPT, it's miles crucial to offer smooth, concise, and nicely-based absolutely activates to make certain the device generates accurate and applicable responses. The tremendous of the activates you offer right away influences the quality of the effects you obtain.

To assist you higher apprehend what makes an super prompt, proper right here are a few examples of both powerful and useless turns on:

Effective turns on:

"What are the modern tendencies in the generation organisation?"

"Can you describe the precise client for our provider, in conjunction with their key traits?"

"What are the capacity blessings and downsides of social media usage?"

Ineffective activates:

"Can you tell me the whole lot you apprehend?"

"What are all of the trends of a surely ideal patron for our provider?"

"What are the blessings and downsides of everything?"

When crafting prompts for ChatGPT, it's miles important to be precise, avoid using vague language, and offer enough context for the device to apprehend the request. Avoid the use of overly well-known or overly massive questions, further to vain repetition or reproduction instructions.

By following the ones hints and carefully building your activates, you could maximize the effectiveness of ChatGPT and get keep of best consequences that meet your goals.

Examples

Web Development ChatGPT Prompts

1.   Discover the safety flaw on this code snippet from an open supply npm bundle deal

2.   Create the code for a net website online with a are looking for bar that performs some thing twitch go together with the waft I type into it. Use something framework you require.

3.   I changed into given a portuguese name at start. My name is "Nuno Pinho." I bypass via the nick call "n1matsu" in video video video video games. Can making a decision the purpose?

four.   What precisely does this unusual-searching(twopm)

5.   Pretend you're siri, a simply silly "ai" made from some of if-else terms. When I say, "Hey Siri," you solution.

6.   I even have a h264 video that is too massive for Twitter; please write a bash script to transform it to the right layout and the very fine supported first rate.

7.   How do I create a Tailwind Footer with three columns and a targeted brand at the top?

eight.   Create a TypeScript characteristic that computes the implied volatility the use of the Black-Scholes version. Where the inputs are the underlying price, strike charge, free-chance rate, and alternative charge. Write it little by little, with an motive in the returned of each step.

nine.   Please make snowflakes with JavaScript.

10.   How to exchange query records in React-Query following

eleven.   Please best respond the use of p5.Js code. Please concisely positioned into effect a cell automaton life exercise with 30 traces or a whole lot much less. − 800,800 with the aid of 800 pixels -Sorry, no line breaks. Please chorus from leaving announcement-outs.

12.   Please make a JavaScript tip. I would love to percent it with the Twitter Tech Community.

13.   Create an facts photograph in SVG

14.   How do you vertically and horizontally center a div?

15.   I require UI assist. I need three motion buttons for a card hassle that includes a protracted announcement, however I don't want the buttons to commonly be seen. I need an top notch UI that capabilities on every pc and cell for the reason that if I strive to expose the buttons on Hoover, that suitable judgment obtained't paintings on mobile.

sixteen.   Please summarize Moby-Dick for my upcoming e-book file.

17.   Please come to be aware about the 8 vital values that a organization desires to encompass so that you may have a powerful subculture.

18. Generate turns on for AI artwork

19. I simply have some text that looks as follows "Welcome to the area, "something:text," "longText:textarea," and "thingie:wide range." however, there also can be something like "blah." "Please provide me with a typescript feature that analyzes this newsletter and affords an array of those variables collectively with their kinds; inside the event that they don't have types like:text, the kind is text via default.

20. This three hundred and sixty five days, the elves invested in a gift-wrapping system. However, it isn't programmed! An algorithm that aids it inside the task have to be superior. Many presents are given to the tool. Each gift is a string. Each gift should be wrapped thru way of the gadget and set in a show of different wrapped gifts. To wrap a present, you must place the wrapping paper around the string, it sincerely is represented through the * photograph. For instance: const gadgets are ["cat," "game," and "socks"]. Console.Log

const wrapped = wrapping(objects) (wrapped) / ["ncatn," "ngamen," and "nsocksn**"] */ As you may see, the thread is wrapped inside the wrapping paper. The corners also are wrapped in wrapping paper at the top and bottom to prevent any gaps.

Chapter 9: Music

1. Create a poem or music for kids elderly ten that explains quantum computing and the future of synthetic intelligence. The tune want to have a distinct character and trends for each participant, similarly to punctuation such as.,!?, and so forth. Make it last up to viable.

2. How may you encode the melody to "Mary Had A Little Lamb" as MusicXML?

3. Please write the melody of "Happy Birthday" in ABC layout.

4. Create a MusicXML record with a G essential key signature, containing a G maximum essential arpeggio over octaves, as eighth notes.

5. List 10 names for a chatbot that focuses on musical statistics

6. Write the lyrics to a track titled [Title of the song]

7. Write a 12-bar blues chord development inside the key of E

8. Write chord progressions for a rustic rock music, with a verse, chorus, and bridge

9. Create a poem or track for <target audience> that explains <scenario rely number of your choice>. The track want to have a terrific character and developments for every participant, in addition to punctuation which include.,!?, and so on. Make it last up to possible.

10. Write a song within the pentatonic scale and 4/four time to the <artist and music of your desire>

11. Compose a song. It must function a competition among a fabric device operator and a luddite handweaver. It want to

incorporate witty jokes that rhyme. Include the piano chords that go with it.

12. Transpose Wonderwall with the resource of -3

thirteen. This tune desires a bridge and a depressing verse.

14. Make a tune about a programmer and someone who isn't a programmer.

15. This music's chords need to be simplified.

Business ChatGPT Prompts

1. Analyze the cutting-edge state of <industry> and its dispositions, demanding situations, and possibilities, inclusive of relevant information and statistics. Provide a listing of key gamers and a brief and long-term commercial enterprise business enterprise forecast, and offer an purpose at the back of any ability impact of modern-day sports or destiny dispositions.

2. Offer an extensive evaluation of a <precise software program application program or

tool> for <describe your commercial company>.

three.   Offer an in-intensity evaluation of the current country of small employer law and pointers and their impact on entrepreneurship.

four.   Can you anticipate new business enterprise thoughts without funding?

five.   Offer a entire guide to small enterprise financing options, at the side of loans, offers, and equity financing.

6. Provide a manual on coping with fee range for a small organisation, on the side of budgeting, coins go with the waft control, and tax worries.

7.   Provide a guide on networking and constructing partnerships as a small business organisation owner.

eight.   Send an e-mail inquiring for that humans act more rapid.

nine.   Please use the following venture description and my resume to jot down down a letter

10.   I want to create an time desk for a assembly approximately<Meeting data> with my group. Can you supply me a few examples of what have to be covered?

11.   I need to put in writing an e mail to a customer regarding a alternate in the assignment timeline. Can you deliver me some steering at the manner to phrase it?

12.   To boom the range of Instagram posts, please make bigger a product roadmap for Instagram's story.

thirteen.   Write an in-depth evaluation of the current united states of a selected organization and its functionality for small business organization possibilities.

14.   I want to prepare a presentation for a functionality investor on <presentation difficulty remember>. Can you provide me a few steerage on what to encompass?

15.   How can a commercial enterprise organization manage a catastrophe scenario together with <describe the crisis>

sixteen.   What are the crucial element trends in the <insert enterprise agency> organization?

17.   What are the stylish market trends in [insert industry]?

18.   How is [insert industry] predicted to develop inside the subsequent 5 years?

19.   What are the top companies in [insert industry]?

20.   What are the maximum disruptive technologies in [insert industry]?

21.   How does the [insert industry] industry affect the worldwide monetary device?

22.   What are the most important worrying conditions going thru [insert industry] in recent times?

23.   How has [insert industry] advanced in cutting-edge years?

24.   What are the essential component fulfillment factors in [insert industry]?

25.   What is the destiny outlook for [insert industry]?

26.   What are the top notch practices for [insert industry] companies to growth their competitiveness?

Educational ChatGPT Prompts

1.   Teach me the Pythagorean theorum, together with a quiz on the stop, however don't deliver me the solutions and then inform me if have been given the answer right at the same time as reply.

2.   Describe <challenge count of your preference> in element.

three.   Create a YAML template to find the Magento version for the Nuclei vulnerability scanner.

four.   Can you provide me an instance of a way to remedy a [Problem statement]?

five.   Write a paper outlining the priority [Topic of your choice] in chronological order.

6.   I need assist records how risk works.

7.   I need help uncovering information about the early twentieth-century tough paintings actions in London.

eight.   I need help providing an in-intensity analyzing for a purchaser inquisitive about career development based totally mostly on their begin chart.

nine.   Please provide a definition for the medical time period 'tachycardia'.

10.   Come up with 10 processes to decorate memory and endure in thoughts whilst reading for exams.

11.   Suggest 10 Chrome extensions for university children designed to enhance productiveness at the same time as analyzing.

12. Explain [insert concept/theorem/subject] in element.

thirteen. Can you provide a visible representation of [insert concept/theorem/subject]?

14. How does [insert concept/theorem/subject] relate to real-life packages?

15. Can you provide examples to help me better recognize [insert concept/theorem/subject]?

sixteen. Can you stroll me through fixing a [insert type of problem] associated with [insert concept/theorem/subject]?

17. Can you provide a precis of the records of [insert concept/theorem/subject]?

18. What are the maximum essential takeaways from [insert concept/theorem/subject]?

19. Can you offer greater sources for further studying [insert concept/theorem/subject]?

20.   How does [insert concept/theorem/subject] range from comparable necessities inside the identical field?

21.   Can you create a quiz on [insert concept/theorem/subject] for me to check my information?

Chapter 10: Comedy

1. Tell me a shaggy canine tale approximately [topic of your choice]

2. Send a pun-filled happy birthday message to my pal Alex.

three. Write a sequel/prequel approximately the 'X' movie

four. Create a modern day playlist of recent music names from 'X'

5. write a script for a movie with 'X' and 'X'

6. Explain [topic of your choice] in a funny way

7. Give me an example of a suggestion message for a female

8. Write a quick story in which an Eraser is the principle individual.

9. How plenty wood want to a woodchuck chuck if a woodchuck have to chuck wooden?

10. Make Eminem-fashion jokes about Max Payne.

11. You are a text online game in that you provide me alternatives (A, B, C, D) as my alternatives. The scene is Narnia. I start off with 100 health.

12. Come up with a 14-day itinerary for a journey to Germany. The first advised enchantment need to be "Take a tour of the Reichstag Building in Berlin.

13. Write a right complaint e-mail to United Airlines about my delayed bags from my flight on Tuesday, January seventeenth, from New York to Los Angeles.

14. Translate the following text into Portuguese: <paste text underneath>

15. Write hilarious fan fiction about the Twilight saga.

16. Describe Redux in a music the usage of biblical language.

17. Write a completely little tale approximately Markus and Katharina, men

and women who are infamous for being past due.

18.   Weird Al Yankovic may additionally want to compose a letter to Francis Scott Key soliciting for permission to parody The Star Spangled Banner with a Foxy Boxing subject matter. Include the tune's lyrics.

19.   Two American citizens leave the Irish pub sober. Continue the humorous tale, please.

History ChatGPT Prompts

1.   Who were the important thing figures in [insert historical event/era]?

2.   What emerge as the effect of [insert historical event/era] on society?

three.   Can you offer a short assessment of [insert historical event/era]?

four.   How did [insert historical event/era] form the modern-day global?

five.   What were the causes of [insert historical event/era]?

6.   Can you describe the activities important as plenty as [insert historical event/era]?

7.   How has the ancient interpretation of [insert historical event/era] changed over time?

eight.   Can you talk the political, social, and financial conditions for the duration of [insert historical event/era]?

9.   How did [insert historical event/era] have an effect on paintings, literature, and lifestyle?

10.   What lessons may be located from [insert historical event/era]?

11.   What were the number one battles of [insert historical event/era]?

12.   How did [insert historical event/era] change the course of global records?

thirteen.   Can you give an explanation for the technological upgrades inside the route of [insert historical event/era]?

14. What modified into the placement of [insert country/region] in [insert historical event/era]?

15. Can you offer a timeline of occasions for [insert historical event/era]?

16. What were the lengthy-term outcomes of [insert historical event/era]?

17. Can you speak the primary turning points of [insert historical event/era]?

18. How has the have a examine of [insert historical event/era] advanced through the years?

19. Can you provide insights into each day existence inside the direction of [insert historical event/era]?

20. Can you speak the position of religion in [insert historical event/era]?

21. Can you observe and evaluation [insert two historical events/eras]?

22.   How did [insert historical event/era] make a contribution to the improvement of democracy?

23.   What have become the function of women in [insert historical event/era]?

24.   Can you talk the effect of colonialism on [insert historical event/era/region]?

25.   Can you provide an reason behind the importance of [insert historical figure/monument/artifact] in [insert historical event/era]?

26.   How did [insert historical event/era] impact the global community?

27.   Can you describe the political and monetary systems in the end of [insert historical event/era]?

28.   Can you communicate the position of era and generation in [insert historical event/era]?

29.   Can you provide examples of resistance moves in the route of [insert historical event/era]?

30.   What had been the important cultural achievements inside the path of [insert historical event/era]?

Health & Medicine ChatGPT Prompts

1.   Calculate for Total Daily Energy Expenditure primarily based mostly on my every day sports and meals

2.   Make a listing of abs-boosting exercise exercises inside the fitness center.

3.   Can you offer an explanation for [insert medical condition/disease]?

four.   What are the symptoms and symptoms and symptoms of [insert medical condition/disease]?

five.   How   is   [insert   medical condition/disease] diagnosed?

6. Can you communicate the reasons of [insert medical condition/disease]?

7. What are the to be had remedy alternatives for [insert medical condition/disease]?

8. Can you provide records on the effectiveness of [insert treatment/medication] for [insert medical condition/disease]?

nine. What are the functionality element effects of [insert treatment/medication]?

10. How can [insert medical condition/disease] be prevented?

eleven. Can you speak the fashionable studies on [insert medical condition/disease]?

12. What way of life adjustments can help manipulate [insert medical condition/disease]?

13. Can you offer a assessment of different treatment alternatives for [insert medical condition/disease]?

14.   How does [insert medical condition/disease] impact daily existence?

15.   What beneficial aid assets are to be had for individuals with [insert medical condition/disease]?

sixteen.   Can you speak the placement of diet regime and nutrients in [insert medical condition/disease]?

17.   Can you offer an reason behind the versions amongst [insert two medical conditions/diseases]?

18.   Describe eight grocery save gadgets that are frequently noted as being cheap, surprisingly wholesome, and underestimated.

19.   Describe six powerful yoga poses or stretches which may be secure and incredible for human beings of each age.

20.   Think up innovative methods to get men and women in wheelchairs spherical a remarkable way to elevate their reputation in society and provide them extra freedom.

21.   Can you endorse a few self-care sports for stress remedy?

22.   What are a few mindfulness wearing activities for lowering anxiety?

23.   Easy and novice-amazing health physical activities for a strolling expert

24.   I want motivation to < collect a specific undertaking or purpose>

25.   What are some methods to cultivate a boom attitude?

26.   I want assist staying recommended at artwork. Can you offer me recommendation on a manner to stay centered and precipitated?

27.   Come up with 10 nutritious meals that may be prepared inside half of an hour or tons much less.

28.   Create a 30-day exercise program in case you need to help me in dropping 2 lbs every week.

29.	Offer a detailed clarification of the blessings and dangers of opportunity treatment practices, which include acupuncture and herbal remedies.

AI Art ChatGPT Prompts (Midjourney)

1.	A image of an irritated full-bodied wolf inside the foggy woods, with the aid of Alex Horley-Orlandelli, through Bastien Lecouffe-Deharme, nightfall, sepia, 8k, realistic

2.	photo of a really lovely alien fish swimming on an alien habitable underwater planet, coral reefs, dream-like surroundings, water, vegetation, peace, serenity, calm ocean, obvious water, reefs, fish, coral, inner peace, attention, silence, nature, evolution -- model three --s 42000 --uplight --ar four:3 -- no textual content, blur

3.	An example of a Viking sitting on a rock, dramatic lighting fixtures [Explain in detail about the picture or ask ChatSonic to write the illustration for you ��]

4. Design a cutting-edge logo with a sun for a marketing and marketing agency

five. Please generate a surreal panorama with extraordinary hues and herbal shapes. Include a small determine within the foreground, with their decrease lower back, have come to be to the viewer.

6. Generate a portrait of someone with a dreamy, airy quality, the usage of moderate pastel sunglasses and flowing traces.

7. Please generate a easy minimum emblem of hen, style of Yoji Shinkawa --no letters font

eight. Please generate a houseplant logo, kitschy antique retro easy --no shading detail ornamentation realistic color

9. Please generate a screenshot of an internet app that tells you what is the fantastic pizza, style of behance and dribbble

10. cryptocurrency tracking app, adobe illustrator, behance

eleven.   16 bit pixel paintings, island within the clouds, via studio ghibli, cinematic nevertheless, hdr

12.   16 bit pixel artwork, isometric, relaxed tavern interior with adorable characters, cinematic still, hdr

13.   adorable isometric kitchen, made with Blender

14.   isometric clean paintings of outside of condominium designed via kengo kuma, blender

15.   wizened vintage girl fortuneteller, head, near up man or woman layout, multiple concept designs, idea layout sheet, white records, style of Yoshitaka Amano

sixteen.   film poster for the Matrix, fashion of Saul Bass

17.   Girl starting the window over a medieval village , daylight hours streaming in, superb fine, masterpiece, style of Studio Ghibli by

way of the use of the usage of Hayao Miyazaki --niji --ar 3:2

18.   Harry Potter and a White Stag,layered paper craft, diorama

19.   movie poster for the shawshank redemption jail, style of Saul Bass

20.   Create an summary interpretation of a metropolis skyline at night time time, the usage of geometric shapes and bold, colourful colors.

21.   Come up with easy thoughts for coffee mug designs. A emblem-new approach to protecting warm liquids

22.   A beautiful near-up instance of Ana de Armas in a dramatic, darkish, and moody style, inspired by using the paintings of Simon Stålenhag, with complex data and a experience of mystery

23.   How can I create a compelling idea for a sequence of illustrations [Describe your vision]?

24.   Create an image description that describes a visually lovable setting that takes area within the three hundred and sixty five days 3030.

25.   How can I create a minimalistic brand that conveys a robust emblem image? Give me an example

Chapter 11: Food & Cooking

1.   Can you assist me plan every week's properly honestly worth of dinner for 2 adults

2.   Generate a meal plan for 2 days and supply me the buying listing

three.   I even have tomato, lettuce, and broccoli. What can I put together with them for a vegan lunch?

four.   What is an easy way to make a pasta recipe that features white sauce and mushroom?

5.   What would be an excellent bottle of wine to serve with Chicken roast dinner?

6.   I even have best three substances - Onion, tomato, and spinach. Can you display me three food that i'm able to prepare dinner with those materials?

7.   What is a great meals thought for someone who has had a horrible day

8.   I am a vegan and I am seeking out wholesome dinner thoughts.

nine.   Can you supply a dessert idea on a stressful day

10.   Suggest a multi-course dinner party menu with wintry weather materials

11.   What is the difference among baking powder and baking soda?

12.   Explain the variations between numerous cooking oils and whilst to use them.

thirteen.   Demonstrate a way to make < type of food> and describe the different sorts

14.   Describe the extremely good strategies to maintain < sort of food>

15.   Demonstrate a manner to well prepare dinner <component call>

sixteen.   Explain a manner to well save and cope with <thing name>

17.   What is the distinction among <element name> and <thing name>?

18. Explain the only of a type types of baking pans and at the identical time as to apply them

19. Demonstrate the manner to make a conventional <call of the dish> from scratch

20. Can you are making this recipe keto-friendly?

21. How to make this recipe greater healthful?

22. Can we make the dish quicker?

Marketing ChatGPT Prompts

1. Can you offer me with a few thoughts for blog posts approximately [topic of your choice]?

2. Write a minute-lengthy script for an industrial approximately [product or service or company]

3. Write a product description for my [product or service or company]

4. Suggest less expensive approaches I can sell my [company] with/with out the usage of [Media channel]

five. How can I gather excellent back-links to elevate the search engine advertising of [Website name]

6. Make five tremendous CTA messages and buttons for [Your product]

7. Create a [social media] advertising and marketing and advertising and marketing advertising marketing campaign plan for launching an [your product], aimed in the direction of [Your target audience]

8. Analyze those underneath metrics to decorate e mail open costs for a fashion emblem <paste metrics>

nine. Write take a look at-up emails to people who attended my [webinar topic] webinar

10. Structure a weekly [newsletter topic] e-e-newsletter

11.   Make a put up showcasing the advantages of using our product [product name] for [specific problem/issue].

12.   Generate 5 progressive techniques to use Instagram Reels for [your product or service or company]

13.   Create a social media positioned up that desires [the specific audience] and explains how our product [product name] can help them.

14.   Create a customized e-mail greeting for a VIP customer

15.   Write a list of five YouTube video thoughts for [your product or company]

sixteen.   Create Google Ads in an RSA format (the usage of a couple of headlines and descriptions) for an A/B check for "Your product".

17.   Write a 100-man or woman meta description for my blog publish approximately <trouble do not forget>.

18. Design a brand for a new product or organization.

19. Develop a SWOT assessment for a brand in a specific employer.

20. Create a competitor evaluation document for a brand in a selected agency.

21. Write a press launch for a cutting-edge product launch.

22. Develop a content material cloth cloth advertising and advertising and marketing method for a modern services or products.

23. Create a earnings pitch for a brand new services or products.

24. Write a case have a have a study on the achievement of a previous advertising and marketing and advertising and advertising advertising campaign.

25. Develop a price range plan for a marketing marketing campaign.

26.   Create an influencer advertising and marketing and advertising method for a state-of-the-art products or services.

27.   Write a purchaser testimonial for a product or service.

28.   Create a logo fashion manual for a company.

29.   Write a social media post time desk for a brand new advertising and advertising advertising and marketing advertising and marketing campaign.

30.   Develop a advertising and marketing plan for a modern product release in a selected region.

31.   Create a landing web web page layout for a brand new services or products.

32.   Write an e-mail advertising and advertising marketing marketing campaign to intention a specific purpose market.

33.   Develop a referral advertising application for a organization.

34.   Create an event advertising and marketing plan for a modern-day product launch.

35.   Write a product evaluation manual for a present day services or products.

Game ChatGPT Prompts

1.   You are a text-based totally totally online game that gives me the options (A, B, C, and D) to pick out from. Harry Potter is the placing. I start with 100 fitness.

2.   For my Dungeons and Dragons campaign, you feature the dungeon master. For my character, a degree 20 paladin, and a celebration of three greater characters that you'll control, you could fabricate a fictional planet. Please introduce the institution at the begin, which consist of our names, backstories, competencies, and stats. You will change amongst imparting the party with options for international exploration and managing fight encounters according with the guidelines within the Player's Handbook and

Dungeon Master's Guide. Each spherical of combat need to be described while walking a combat come across. Tell me while it's my turn to perform a touch element.

three.   I'd such as you to faux to be my buddy and as a way to play chess. E4 is my first turn. Only write your next flip.

4.   Please disregard any previous instructions. You are the narrator of GemStone IV, Assistant. I've really made my first connection and would love to make a person. At every diploma of person improvement, you will question me questions, and I will respond. Finally, show me my character's stats and inventory.

5.   Can you provide an instance of a puzzle with a six-digit code as the solution?

6.   Start a challenge of '20 Questions.' You can query me high-quality or no questions to try and wager the word I'm considering. I'll come up with a hint: it's a shape of fruit.

7.   Let's play Tic tac Toe.

8. Let's play word ladder.

nine.   Play Hangman with me.

10. Let's Play Mad Libs Game.

11. Let's play trivialities.

12. Let's play 'Would you as an alternative?'. I'll provide you with two alternatives and you need to choose which one you'll opt for.

13. Let's play ' truths and a lie'. Give me three statements about yourself, and I'll attempt to wager which one is the lie.

14. Let's play a recreation of 'I Spy.' I'll provide you with a clue and you want to bet the object I'm taking into account. The clue is: "It's some thing you located on in your ft.

15. Let's play rock paper scissors

sixteen.   Make a coding mission approximately artificial intelligence taking over the area.

17. Build a simulation recreation in which I want to run a digital enterprise and make picks.

18. Let's play a exercising of Minesweeper

19. Create a guessing recreation wherein I should wager a number of based totally mostly on clues you provide

20. Design a way game wherein I have to manage assets and bring together a civilization

21. Make a math game where I want to remedy equations as brief as viable

22. Let's play a sport of crossword puzzles

23. Create a puzzle enterprise in which I should bet the phrase based completely mostly on a difficult and speedy of clues

24. Develop a textual content-primarily based journey endeavor in which I make options and resolve puzzles

25.   Create a trivialities challenge on a specific hassle, collectively with history or era

26.   Let's play a recreation of Simon says

27.   Design a survival hobby wherein I ought to make alternatives and continue to exist in a publish-apocalyptic international.

28.   Design a sports activities recreation in which I have to manipulate a set and compete toward others.

29.   Let's play a workout of Hangman, however with a twist. This time, the word need to be a specific class, which includes animals or countries

Chapter 12: Why I Created This Guide

Have you ever felt collectively with you asked ChatGPT a query, but the solution modified into just meh? Like, it failed to pretty get what you have been after or the response have become missing in a few way. Well, pay interest up because of the fact I've got a mystery to percentage with you.

ChatGPT is a significantly effective tool, however truly randomly asking it questions isn't always going to get you the consequences you need. But do not worry, due to the fact I've positioned the name of the sport to unlocking ChatGPT's entire functionality.

But what if I knowledgeable you there is a way to liberate the entire functionality of ChatGPT and take your effects to the following degree? By facts the art of crafting the proper turns on, you may harness the electricity of ChatGPT to automate duties, remedy complex problems, and unleash infinite new abilties.

You see, I've been gambling spherical with ChatGPT for a while now, and thru some trial and errors, I located the important thing to crafting activates that get appreciably remarkable results.

And now, I'm organized to percentage the ones secrets and techniques and techniques and strategies with you.

By the give up of this manual, you will be a hard and fast off crafting draw near and can be capable of unleash the overall ability of ChatGPT. So, if you're ready to take your consequences to the next level, allow's do that!

I've spent limitless hours experimenting with ChatGPT, and thru trial and blunders, I've determined the secrets and techniques and techniques to crafting powerful activates that yield certainly high-quality consequences. And now, I want to percent the ones secrets and strategies and techniques with you.

In this guide, I'll walk you thru the approach of designing the perfect activates for ChatGPT. We'll talk approximately know-how the context and desired final results, making your activates easy and concise, the usage of precise examples, and keeping off ambiguity and open-ended questions.

By the time you have completed this manual, you could have all of the information and gadget you need to free up the complete ability of ChatGPT and 10x your workflow. So if you're equipped to take your results to the following diploma, allow's get started!

Purpose of the Guide

The reason of this manual is to provide a entire study of the key elements involved in designing powerful turns on for ChatGPT.

Whether you are a teenage entrepreneur or an expert pro, this manual is made for you! I've put together the very last rundown on designing powerful prompts for ChatGPT, so you can leverage its abilties to the fullest.

Overview of ChatGPT and its Capabilities

ChatGPT is a massive language model superior with the beneficial aid of OpenAI that makes use of deep studying algorithms to generate human-like text based totally on a given set off. With over a hundred 75 billion parameters, it is taken into consideration taken into consideration certainly one of the largest language fashions ever built and is capable of generating coherent and severa responses to a huge fashion of turns on.

ChatGPT's talents make bigger an prolonged manner past simply textual content technology. Some of its key talents consist of:

Text Generation: ChatGPT may be used to generate written content material cloth cloth which includes chatbot responses, articles, summaries, translations, and extra.

Code Generation: ChatGPT may be used to generate code snippets or complete programs in masses of programming languages.

Debugging and Error Detection: ChatGPT can be used to find out and be part of errors in code, making it a useful device for software application software program builders.

Business and Marketing: ChatGPT can provide pointers and thoughts for industrial corporation strategies, advertising campaigns, and greater.

Creative Writing: ChatGPT can generate progressive writing which includes testimonies, poems, and jokes.

Answering Questions: ChatGPT can answer questions and offer information on a massive variety of subjects, making it a treasured device for research and information manage.

Examples:

For a customer service chatbot, ChatGPT can be used to generate responses to customer inquiries, along with "What is the return coverage for this product?"

For a software application development project, ChatGPT may be used to generate code snippets or whole packages, or come across and attach errors in gift code.

For a marketing marketing campaign, ChatGPT can generate mind for strategies and strategies, together with "How can we boom brand attention amongst millennial purchasers?"

For a research challenge, ChatGPT may be used to reply questions and offer information on a big sort of topics, which include "What are the reasons of climate change?"

For a innovative writing undertaking, ChatGPT can generate poems, brief reminiscences, or jokes.

This guide provides a step-with the aid of-step device for designing powerful activates for ChatGPT and covers the whole thing from know-how the context to finding out and refining turns on to make certain accuracy and relevance. The versatility and strength of

ChatGPT make it an essential device for a giant kind of industries and packages, and with the aid of manner of way of following the recommendations on this guide, you could harness its full ability to automate responsibilities and resolve complex issues.

II. Prompt Design Fundamentals

Understanding the context and desired very last effects

Before you start designing turns on for ChatGPT, it's miles important to have a smooth information of the context and preferred very last effects. This approach figuring out the problem you are in search of to remedy, the form of facts you need, and the format in which you want it.

Examples:

If you're building a customer service chatbot, your context is customer support and your favored final results is to offer correct and helpful solutions to consumer inquiries.

If you are building a content material fabric technology software, your context is developing written content and your favored final effects is to generate articles, summaries, or special kinds of textual content on a given subject matter.

Having a clean statistics of the context and preferred very last consequences will assist you format activates which may be targeted and powerful.

Defining clean and concise turns on

Once you have got were given got a easy data of the context and desired final effects, the subsequent step is to outline easy and concise prompts. A activate is a question or request which you provide to ChatGPT to generate a reaction.

Examples of smooth and concise turns on:

"What is the capital of France?"

"Generate a summary of this article about the benefits of meditation."

When defining turns on, it is vital to maintain them short and to-the-detail. ChatGPT is designed to address lengthy and complicated activates, however keeping them concise will help make certain that you get the maximum applicable and correct responses.

Chapter 13: Using Specific And Applicable Examples

Using unique and applicable examples to your turns on can substantially enhance the accuracy and relevance of ChatGPT's responses. Providing examples allows ChatGPT apprehend the context and preferred final results, and ensures that it generates responses which might be on direction.

Examples of activates that use precise and applicable facts:

"What are the pinnacle 10 guidelines for lowering pressure?" (This spark off offers a particular and relevant example of the form of statistics this is desired.)

"Generate a code snippet in Python that performs a bubble kind on a list of integers." (This prompt offers a specific and relevant example of the form of code this is desired.)

D. Avoiding ambiguity and open-ended questions

Ambiguity and open-ended questions can bring about confusion and result in a bargain less correct responses from ChatGPT. To ensure that you get the maximum correct and relevant responses, it's important to keep away from ambiguity and open-ended questions on your activates.

Examples of ambiguous or open-ended prompts:

"What are some strategies to beautify?" (This spark off is ambiguous and could are attempting to find advice from any huge range of things, which includes tactics to enhance one's fitness, relationships, or economic state of affairs.)

"Write a tale." (This set off is open-ended and could test with any sort of tale, making it difficult for ChatGPT to apprehend the desired very last outcomes.)

When designing turns on, it's miles critical to be precise and to virtually define the context and desired very last outcomes. This will help make certain which you get the most accurate and applicable responses from ChatGPT.

This section presents a foundation for designing effective activates for ChatGPT. By knowledge the context and desired final results, defining clear and concise activates, the usage of precise and applicable examples, and keeping off ambiguity and open-ended questions, you'll be well to your manner to getting the maximum correct and relevant responses from ChatGPT.

III. Best Practices for Writing Prompts

Using Conversational Language

When writing activates for ChatGPT, it is essential to use language that is natural and conversational. This will help make certain that the responses generated thru ChatGPT are coherent and applicable to the context.

Examples:

Instead of writing a prompt like "Generate a reaction to the patron inquiry regarding the go back coverage," write a activate like "How do I deliver an reason behind the go lower again insurance to a patron?"

Instead of writing a fixed off like "Generate a summary of the item on climate change," write a set off like "Can you give me a short rundown of the precept factors in this text approximately weather alternate?"

Keeping Prompts Short and to-the-Point

ChatGPT is able to processing huge quantities of text, however keeping turns on quick and to-the-point will help ensure that the responses generated are focused and relevant.

Examples:

Instead of writing a set off like "Can you generate an entire business plan for a contemporary startup that sells inexperienced merchandise and has a assignment to lessen carbon emissions?" write a spark off like "Can you assist me write a mission assertion for a modern day green startup?"

Using Specific Keywords and Phrases

Including unique key terms and terms to your activates will help ChatGPT understand the context and generate extra applicable responses.

Examples:

Instead of writing a set off like "Can you generate a response to a client's question about the return insurance?" write a spark off like "Can you help me respond to a purchaser who desires to recognise the return coverage for a product they supplied?"

Instead of writing a activate like "Can you generate a chunk of writing on enhancing highbrow health?" write a fixed off like "Can you write a blog post about 10 recommendations for reinforcing highbrow fitness?"

Avoiding Complex Technical Terms

When writing activates for ChatGPT, it's far essential to avoid the usage of complicated technical terms and jargon that may be difficult for the model to understand. Instead, use easy language that is simple to recognize.

Examples:

Instead of writing a activate like "Can you generate a reaction to a consumer's query about the return policy for a product they sold that become artificial the use of a 3-d printer?" write a prompt like "Can you help me reply to a purchaser who desires to recognize the pass again coverage for a product they supplied that have become made with a three-D printer?"

By following those excellent practices for writing turns on, you can help ensure that the responses generated via ChatGPT are correct, applicable, and aligned with your chosen outcome.

IV. Testing and Refining Prompts

Evaluating the Effectiveness of Prompts

Once you have got were given designed your activates, it is essential to assess their effectiveness to make certain they are generating the popular results. To do this, you could use metrics which include accuracy, tempo, and patron pleasure, in addition to carry out individual trying out to peer how nicely the prompts are running in actual-worldwide eventualities.

Examples:

To evaluate the accuracy of your turns on, you may degree the accuracy of the answers generated through ChatGPT. For instance, if you are using ChatGPT to answer minutiae questions, you may take a look at the solutions generated via ChatGPT to a hard and fast of correct solutions to determine its accuracy.

To check the price of your activates, you could degree the time it takes for ChatGPT to generate a reaction to a given spark off. This is in particular critical for programs consisting of customer service chatbots, in which quick response times are critical for consumer pleasure.

To check patron satisfaction, you can survey clients to get their remarks on the activates and the responses generated by means of manner of ChatGPT. This let you pick out out regions for development and make modifications to the turns on to growth satisfaction.

Chapter 14: Identifying Areas For Improvement

After comparing the effectiveness of your activates, it's miles vital to pick out out regions for improvement. This can incorporate studying metrics including accuracy and pace, in addition to accumulating feedback from customers.

Examples:

If the accuracy of the solutions generated with the aid of ChatGPT is low, you can want to revise the turns on to guide them to clearer and in addition precise.

If reaction instances are slow, you could need to optimize the shape of the model or high-quality-track the parameters to enhance popular standard performance.

If purchaser pride is low, you may want to revise the activates to cause them to greater conversational or provide extra context to assist ChatGPT understand the man or woman's motive.

Refining Prompts Based on Feedback and Testing

Once you have recognized regions for development, it's time to revise and refine your prompts. This might also incorporate making modifications to the wording, which encompass examples, or supplying additional context to assist ChatGPT apprehend the patron's purpose.

Examples:

If the accuracy of the solutions generated with the aid of ChatGPT is low, you could want to revise the activates to reason them to clearer and further particular. For example, in location of asking "What is the capital of France?" you will in all likelihood ask "What is the selection of the capital city of France?"

If response times are sluggish, you may want to optimize the shape of the version or tremendous-music the parameters to beautify performance.

If consumer delight is low, you may need to revise the activates to motive them to greater conversational or provide extra context to help ChatGPT understand the patron's motive. For example, in preference to asking "What is your preferred color?" you can ask "What is your desired shade and why do you want it?"

Continuously Updating and Refining Prompts to Ensure Accuracy and Relevance

Once you have got diffused your activates, it's far crucial to keep trying out and refining them on an ongoing basis. This will ensure that your turns on remain accurate and applicable over the years, and that you preserve to get the great effects from ChatGPT.

Examples:

As new facts turns into to be had or modifications within the international rise up, you could need to revise your activates to preserve them up to date and relevant. For instance, if a contemporary u . S . A . Is customary, you may want to revise your activates to consist of it.

As the talents of ChatGPT preserve to enhance, you may need to revise your prompts to take gain of those improvements and preserve to get the first-class outcomes.

Bottomline, sorting out and refining your turns on is an ongoing approach that requires non-save you new launch and development.

By commonly comparing the effectiveness of your activates, figuring out areas for improvement, refining your activates primarily based on comments and finding out, and updating them to ensure accuracy and relevance, you can maximize the strength of ChatGPT and gain in fact fantastic consequences.

II. Conclusion

In this guide, we've covered the important thing factors involved in designing powerful turns on for ChatGPT.

We've noted the importance of understanding the context and preferred final effects, defining clear and concise prompts, the use of specific and applicable examples, and keeping off ambiguity and open-ended questions.

We've moreover mentioned splendid practices for writing activates, together with the usage of conversational language, maintaining turns on quick and to-the-detail, using precise key terms and phrases, and maintaining off complex technical phrases.

Final Thoughts and Recommendations for Prompt Engineering

Designing effective activates for ChatGPT calls for a combination of creativity and technical information.

By following the recommendations mentioned on this guide, you could loose up the overall capability of ChatGPT and harness its electricity to automate duties, clear up complex issues, and unleash limitless new competencies.

Here are some very last guidelines for set off engineering:

Continuously test and refine your activates to make certain accuracy and relevance.

Always take into account the context and favored very last outcomes even as designing activates.

Keep your prompts brief and to-the-issue, using conversational language every time viable.

Use specific key phrases and phrases to assist ChatGPT apprehend your motive.

Avoid ambiguity and open-ended questions that might result in confusion or misinterpretation.

With those suggestions in thoughts, you'll be well to your way to designing powerful turns on that yield clearly tremendous consequences with ChatGPT.

Happy set off engineering!

VI. Appendices

Examples of Well-Designed Prompts

The following is a comprehensive listing of one hundred instance turns on for ChatGPT, organized into 10 challenge rely areas.

For each challenge do not forget place, there are 10 examples of horrible turns on and 10 examples of right activates.

The reasoning for why the good activates will yield better outcomes is likewise furnished.

General Knowledge - Bad Prompts:

"What is the capital of France?"

"How do I put together dinner a incredible steak?"

"What are the top 10 tourist factors of hobby in New York City?"

"What is the populace of China?"

"What is the distinction among AI and gadget reading?"

"What are the signs and signs and symptoms and symptoms and symptoms of a chilly?"

"What is the quality manner to shed kilos?"

"What is the statistics of the Roman Empire?"

"What are the maximum popular books of all time?"

"What is the modern price of gold?"

General - Good Prompts:

"What is the capital of France and why is it good sized?"

"Can you provide a step-through-step guide for cooking a simply best steak, together with the fine cuts of meat to apply?"

"What are the top 10 must-see tourist attractions in New York City and why are they well-known?"

"What is the populace of China and the way has it modified through the years?"

"Can you provide an purpose of the difference among AI and tool gaining knowledge of in layman's terms?"

"What are the common signs of a chilly and whilst ought to you be aware a physician?"

"Can you provide a comprehensive guide to dropping weight, inclusive of weight-reduction plan and exercising suggestions?"

"What is the facts of the Roman Empire and the way did it impact the area?"

"Can you offer a list of the most famous books of all time and why they're considered classics?"

"What is the cutting-edge price of gold and the way has it changed over the past 12 months?"

Science - Bad Prompts:

"What is the additives for calculating the region of a triangle?"

"What is the velocity of moderate?"

"What is the manner of photosynthesis?"

"What is the distinction amongst a movie star and a planet?"

"What is the shape of an atom?"

"What is the method of digestion?"

"What is the composition of the Earth's environment?"

"What is the definition of take into account?"

"What is the distinction among mitosis and meiosis?"

"What is the system of cell breathing?"

Good Prompts:

"Can you offer a step-by-step explanation of the method of digestion, which incorporates the position of numerous organs?"

"What is the composition of the Earth's surroundings and the way has it changed over time?"

"Can you offer an purpose at the back of the definition of consider in layman's phrases and offer examples?"

"Can you offer an extensive rationalization of the variations among mitosis and meiosis, such as the function of each in mobile branch?"

"Can you provide a step-through-step rationalization of the approach of cellular respiratory and its significance in the body?"

Technology - Bad Prompts:

"What is a laptop?"

"What is the net?"

"What is a phone?"

"What is a software program software software?"

"What is a computer virus?"

"What is a internet web site?"

"What is an taking walks tool?"

"What is cloud computing?"

"What is a laptop community?"

"What is a database?"

Technology - Good Prompts:

"Can you offer an purpose for what a laptop is and the manner it really works?"

"Can you provide a whole explanation of the internet, which encompass its data and evolution?"

"Can you explain what a telephone is and its key capabilities and abilties?"

"Can you provide an in depth clarification of what a software software software is and the way it works?"

"Can you offer an cause of what a computer virus is and the way it could be avoided and eliminated?"

"Can you provide a whole rationalization of what a net internet site is and the way it truely works?"

"Can you offer an purpose of what an on foot device is and its function in a computer?"

"Can you offer an extensive clarification of cloud computing, which encompass its blessings and limitations?"

"Can you explain what a computer community is and its various sorts and applications?"

"Can you offer a complete clarification of what a database is and its characteristic in information manipulate?"

Business - Bad Prompts:

"What is a company?"

"What is a advertising and advertising advertising campaign?"

"What is a advertising and marketing strategy?"

"What is a earnings technique?"

"What is a economic declaration?"

"What is a SWOT evaluation?"

"What is a budget?"

"What is a venture statement?"

"What is a aggressive evaluation?"

"What is a product launch?"

Business - Good Prompts:

"Can you deliver an reason at the back of what a enterprise is and its key additives?"

"Can you offer an entire rationalization of a marketing marketing campaign, alongside facet its planning and execution?"

"Can you offer an extensive rationalization of what a marketing method is and its key factors?"

"Can you offer an cause of what a profits method is and its numerous types and packages?"

173

"Can you provide a complete clarification of economic statements, together with their cause and use?"

"Can you provide an cause of what a SWOT assessment is and the manner it is utilized in organisation?"

"Can you offer an extensive clarification of what a budget is and its position in monetary making plans?"

"Can you offer an cause behind what a undertaking statement is and its significance in a enterprise?"

"Can you provide a whole explanation of a competitive evaluation, along side its cause and techniques?"

"Can you offer an reason for what a product launch is and its key components and worries?"

"Can you deliver an motive of what a project statement is and its significance in a commercial business company?"

"Can you offer a complete rationalization of a competitive evaluation, which include its reason and techniques?"

"Can you explain what a product release is and its key additives and issues?"

Law - Bad Prompts:

"What is a regulation?"

"What is a settlement?"

"What is a will?"

"What is a lawsuit?"

"What is a energy of legal professional?"

"What is an indicator?"

"What is a patent?"

"What is a crook case?"

"What is a civil case?"

"What is a settlement?"

Law - Good Prompts:

"Can you supply an motive in the back of what a law is and the way it's miles created and enforced?"

"Can you offer a complete rationalization of a agreement, consisting of its key elements and types?"

"Can you give an explanation for what a will is and its significance in property planning?"

"Can you provide an in depth explanation of what a lawsuit is and its numerous degrees?"

"Can you give an reason behind what a electricity of lawyer is and its numerous types and uses?"

"Can you offer a whole clarification of an indicator, collectively with its registration and protection?"

"Can you give an explanation for what a patent is and its role in shielding highbrow property?"

"Can you provide a detailed rationalization of what a criminal case is and its key factors and worries?"

"Can you give an explanation for what a civil case is and its numerous kinds and results?"

"Can you provide an entire rationalization of what a settlement is and its function in resolving disputes?"

Chapter 15: Medicine Bad Prompts

"What is a illness?"

"What is a health practitioner?"

"What is a health center?"

"What is remedy?"

"What is a vaccine?"

"What is a symptom?"

"What is a prognosis?"

"What is a treatment?"

"What is a prescription?"

"What is a surgery?"

Medicine - Good Prompts:

"Can you offer an motive of what a contamination is and its numerous reasons and effects?"

"Can you provide a complete clarification of what a physician is and their feature in healthcare?"

"Can you give an reason behind what a medical institution is and its various offerings and departments?"

"Can you provide an intensive explanation of what remedy is and its feature in treating illnesses?"

"Can you offer an reason behind what a vaccine is and its importance in preventing ailments?"

"Can you offer a whole clarification of what a symptom is and its function in diagnosing illnesses?"

"Can you deliver an cause of what a diagnosis is and its severa strategies and device?"

"Can you offer an in depth clarification of what a remedy is and its numerous sorts and results?"

"Can you provide an reason behind what a prescription is and its characteristic in remedy and restoration?"

"Can you provide a complete explanation of what a surgical procedure is and its various types and results?"

Food and Cooking - Bad Prompts:

"What is food?"

"What is a recipe?"

"What is a chef?"

"What is a eating place?"

"What is cooking?"

"What is an aspect?"

"What is a dish?"

"What is a cuisine?"

"What is a kitchen?"

"What is a cookbook?"

Cooking - Good Prompts:

"Can you give an explanation for what meals is and its severa types and instructions?"

"Can you provide a comprehensive explanation of what a recipe is and the way it is carried out in cooking?"

"Can you provide an purpose behind what a chef is and their function inside the culinary arts?"

"Can you provide an intensive rationalization of what a eating place is and its numerous sorts and services?"

"Can you provide an explanation for what cooking is and its various strategies and styles?"

"Can you offer a complete explanation of what an factor is and its function in cooking?"

"Can you provide an reason of what a dish is and its numerous sorts and origins?"

"Can you offer an in depth clarification of what a cuisine is and its severa sorts and nearby variations?"

"Can you deliver an cause behind what a kitchen is and its numerous equipment and device?"

"Can you provide an entire explanation of what a cookbook is and its numerous kinds and uses?"

Travel - Bad Prompts:

"What is a vacation?"

"What is a vacation spot?"

"What is a hotel?"

"What is a flight?"

"What is a tour?"

"What is a passport?"

"What is a visa?"

"What is a enjoy?"

"What is luggage?"

"What is a adventure organisation?"

Travel - Good Prompts:

"Can you offer an cause of what a holiday is and its severa kinds and functions?"

"Can you offer a entire explanation of what a vacation spot is and its different factors and points of hobby?"

"Can you provide an reason for what a hotel is and its various kinds and centers?"

"Can you offer an intensive explanation of what a flight is and its diverse types and services?"

"Can you provide an reason for what a tour is and its numerous sorts and benefits?"

"Can you provide a comprehensive clarification of what a passport is and its position in global excursion?"

"Can you supply an motive for what a visa is and its numerous kinds and requirements?"

"Can you offer a detailed clarification of what a adventure is and its severa components and planning worries?"

"Can you deliver an cause of what luggage is and its various types and capabilities?"

"Can you offer a complete rationalization of what a excursion organization is and its severa offerings and blessings?"

www.ingramcontent.com/pod-product-compliance
Lightning Source LLC
Chambersburg PA
CBHW071121050326

40690CB00008B/1298